Pearson's Canal Companion
KENNET & AVON
River Thames Oxford - Brentford

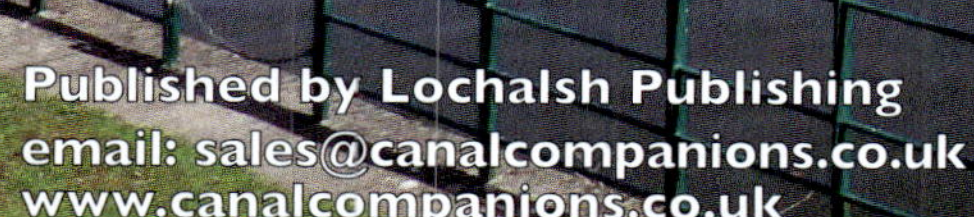

Published by Lochalsh Publishing
email: sales@canalcompanions.co.uk
www.canalcompanions.co.uk

Copyright: Lochalsh Publishing
Third Edition 2012
Updated 2015/17/21
ISBN 978 0 9562777 6 3

GRAPPLING with my Census form, I hesitate momentarily when it comes to 'Occupation?', before settling for 'Guidebook Compiler'. That'll fox 'em, I chuckle; though somehow doubting if anyone - just as 'What's My Line?' confounding as I - ever bothers to scrutinize the answers that we give.

"Oh, what a lovely job!" a woman gushed, on the otherwise empty platform of Acton Bridge railway station, at the end of a long hot day's tramp along the banks of the Weaver Navigation. And I could scarcely demur, remembering another occasion at Crewe, where I was loitering, informally dressed in T-shirt and shorts, in wait for a train to take me up to Cumbria for a day of island-hopping off the Furness coast. In contrast, on the opposite platform, sharp-suited businessmen jostled to board a Euston-bound express. Naturally, they would make far more money than me. But would they have the wisdom to spend it rewardingly?

"How do you get a job like that?" a fellow lock-wheeler once enviously enquired, as we stuggled with the recalcitrant worm gear of a lock on the outskirts of Solihull. Well, failing English and Geography at A Level certainly went someway to kick-starting my career. Had I passed, I would undoubtedly have a greater appreciation of Jane Austen and John Donne, together with the imports and exports of Uruguay, and the recessional moraines of the English Lakes. Far better, in my case, to be familiar with the minutiae of E. Temple Thurston and William Bliss, the trolleybus network of South Lancashire, and the Witham Navigable Drains. No, with the benefit of hindsight, it was not so much that I failed my exams, more that the syllabus failed me.

With a book token presented to me on the occasion of my twenty-first birthday - an event marked happily, in splendid isolation, by the consumption of a Holland's of Baxenden meat and potato pie - I acquired a copy of Henry Thorold's and Jack Yates's *Lincolnshire - A Shell Guide*. As

a template for guidebook compilation it could hardly be bettered. It has been joined, down the years, by in excess of thirty other Shell Guides, and I treasure them all dearly, yet, like a first love, Lincolnshire remains the one most precious to me. Thorold, it transpired, was an eccentric country squire, a chaplain at Lancing College, and the proud owner of a 1951 Bentley, in which much of his research was swash-bucklingly undertaken. As a role model, he left nothing to be desired. And if I couldn't emulate his panache, I could at least be inspired by his thorough approach; 'thorough', funnily enough, being how he insisted his surname should be pronounced.

Nature or nurture, then? I'm inclined to the former. I believe I was born to the breed, there being a good deal of the 'train-spotter' in my psyche, a collector of facts and figures, a stickler for precision. When training to be a guidebook compiler, it helps enormously if one has a tendency to fall in love with places as opposed to people. Not that I consider myself a misanthrope. On the contrary, I cherish all my fellow human beings ... on the tacit understanding they keep their distance. Places, places, places; they are what have kept me motivated down the decades. And, frankly, it hardly matters whether I arrive by boat, or bus, or bicycle - or hot air balloon, for that matter - it is the frisson of the encounter that enthralls.

The ensuing Census question - 'How Long Have You Been In Your Present Employment?' proved somewhat easier to answer. A nice round number: '40 Years.' Little wonder then, that, in common with Nick Carraway, narrator - as any syllabus-embracing A Level candidate will tell you - of F. Scott Fitzgerald's *The Great Gatsby*, I find myself being 'borne back ceaselessly into the past.' Fortunately for me, that's precisely where I am at my most content. And equally fortunately for you, fellow travellers, there is no better way of getting there than by inland waterway.

Contents

Kennet & Avon Canal
Bristol - Reading
Maps 1 - 21 Pages 4 - 38

Gallery
Pages 39 - 47

River Thames
Oxford - Brentford
Maps 22 - 43 Pages 48 - 90

Information
Pages 91 - 93

Boating Directory
Pages 94 - 95

ENVY the lucky boater who has to begin or end their voyage in the superbly atmospheric setting of Bristol's Floating Harbour. Though bear in mind that it is the vessels which 'float' and not the docks; unless, that is, you've imbibed prodigiously on too many of the city's admirable microbrewed ales.

Early in the 19th century William Jessop designed a new enclosed harbour to eradicate difficulties involved in loading and unloading vessels at the mercy of the River Avon's considerable tides. But Bristol's maritime tradition goes back much further than this, and many a fortune was acquired in the 'triangular trade': guns to Africa; slaves to America; sugar, rum, tobacco and cotton back. Coastal trade was also an important tradition. The quayside at Welsh Back -

now reminiscent of Amsterdam in its cobbled, tree-lined ambience - once reverberated to the clamour of Welsh voices whose owners had sailed over in trows with cargoes of slate and stone and coal. Beyond Bristol Bridge, George's brewery (converted into apartments and offices now) was formerly a busy user of water transport as well, whilst the importing of sherry was another activity closely associated with the port of Bristol. Trade ceased in the Floating Harbour in the 1970s but it doesn't take too much imagination to picture the vibrant scenes of the past which characterised it during the city's mercantile heyday.

In the absence of one's own boat it is still easy to explore the city centre by water courtesy of the frequent ferries which operate all the way from Temple Quay in the east (adjacent to Temple Meads railway station) to Cumberland Basin in the west (by the entrance lock to the tidal Avon). The best public moorings for visiting boaters are to be found on a pontoon just west of Prince Street Bridge.

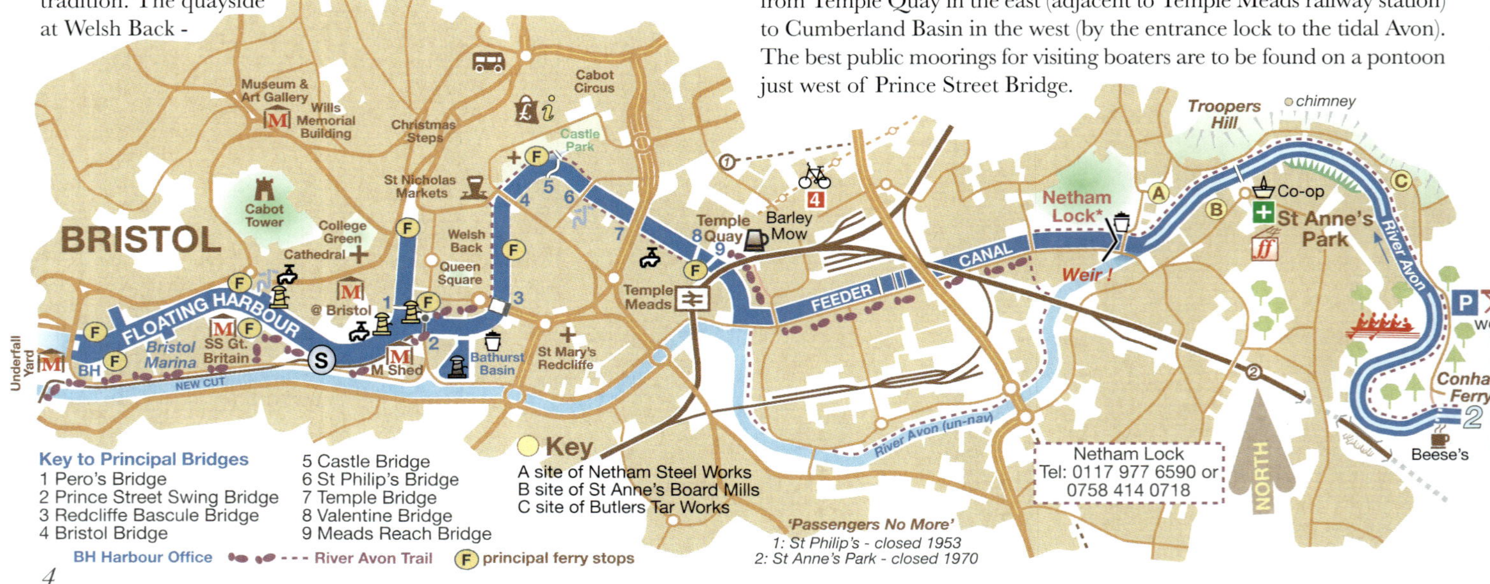

They offer handy and rapid access to the city centre. Both Prince Street Swing and the neighbouring Redcliffe Bascule bridges have sufficient headroom for most inland waterway craft without needing to be swung or raised respectively.

Walkways - more or less intact on either bank - permit pedestrian exploration of the Floating Harbour. Here and there, railway tracks remain in situ, creating an atmosphere of days gone by when much transhipment occurred. Sadly all the lines have been uprooted on the north side of the harbour where signs used to advise drivers to desist from shunting during periods when services were being held in the adjoining Cathedral.

How nice it would be to return to those days. In the mid Fifties something in the region of ten thousand ships per annum were visiting the Port of Bristol, though the larger vessels involved used the docks at Portishead and Avonmouth, as their dimensions precluded passage upstream through the restrictive Avon Gorge, where the tidal range was close to fifty feet. The City Docks hosted the coastal and continental trade, vessels up to a maximum of about fifteen hundred tons. Many traded from the Baltic and Scandinavia with timber and woodpulp for Bristol's paper-makers. From warmer climes came wine from Portugal, Spanish grapefruits and South African oranges.

Passing beneath the phalanx of railway tracks which form the northern approach to Temple Meads station, boaters make their way out of the city along the Feeder Canal as far as Netham Lock. This is not a particularly salubrious part of the city in terms of general appearance, indeed it was once more heavily industrialised, notably with the presence of Lysaght's Ironworks, the Great Western Cotton Factory and Netham Chemical Company, all heavy users of water transport.

Depending on tide levels, Netham Lock may well be open to pass through without operating, but it would be sensible to telephone ahead and apprise the lock-keeper of your approach.

Once through the lock steer well clear of the weir which takes the Avon downstream towards the open sea. Useful shopping facilities are available at St Anne's Park, though you may have to improvise when mooring and this is definitely not a spot for a lengthy stay. Housing has replaced the site of Butlers Tar Works, originally established by Isambard Kingdom Brunel to produce creosote with which to protect the wooden sleepers of his Great Western Railway. Steve Grudgings described the works and other local industries in *Archive* issues 108/9. Soon, however, the scenery improves dramatically, as the river winds through a deepening gorge where regenerated woodland has healed industrial scars. There are glimpses of Brunel's decorated tunnel portals before Conham Ferry, operated by the owners of Beese's charming tea gardens.

Incidentally, when boating inbound to Bristol, it's a good idea to acquire a copy of Bristol Harbour's information booklet from the keeper at Netham, as it elaborates on the information we have space to publish here.

Bristol Map 1

Bristol is a scintillating city, full of atmospheric passages and corners, alleyways and stairways, as befits a former sea-trading port. Though much damage was wrought by bombing raids during the Second World War, a sense of unity has been restored, and the melding of old and new has been arguably more successful here than in, say Plymouth or Coventry. Two magnificent churches cry out for your attention, the Cathedral and St Mary's, Redcliffe. Elizabeth I described the latter as the fairest church in England. But it is the Floating Harbour which renders Bristol unique, and whose perspective defines the city's rich history.

Eating & Drinking

BARLEY MOW - Barton Road (NE of Temple Quay). Tel: 0117 930 4709. Bristol is home to several excellent microbreweries and this is the flagship pub of one of the best, Bristol Beer Factory. Open from noon daily. Lunch and evening food. BS2 0LF

BEESE'S - Conham. Tel: 0117 977 7412. Charming riverside bar and tea garden dating from 1846 and eponymously named after a ferryman and his wife who laid on teas. Moorings for customers. BS4 4SX

CASAMIA - Lower Guinea Street. (adjacent Bathurst Basin). Tel: 0117 959 2884. Michelin starred trattoria open for lunch Fri & Sat and dinner Wed-Sat. BS1 6SY

FISH - Welsh Back. Tel: 0117 929 0704. Floating seafood restaurant by Bristol Bridge. BS1 4SB *continued overleaf* continued from page 5:

HARBOUR HOUSE - The Grove. Tel: 0117 925 1212. Stylish wooden-built restaurant said to have been IKB's personal boat house. BS1 4RB

MUD DOCK - The Grove. Tel: 0117 332 3971. Zany cafe/restaurant and bike shop/repair station. Open from 10am (9am Sat). BS1 4RB

RIVERSTATION - The Grove. Tel: 0117 914 4434. Contemporary restaurant/bar with harbourside al-fresco terraces. BS1 4RB

THREE BROTHERS BURGERS - Welsh Back. Tel: 0117 927 7050. Beer & burgers afloat from noon. BS1 4SB

Shopping

There are lively Harbourside Markets each weekend, but you should also beat a path to the St Nicholas Markets (reminiscent of Oxford's equally wonderful indoor market - Map 22), just west of Bristol Bridge. Many independent traders rub shoulders with better known chains in Bristol's Shopping Quarter. Christmas Steps is a centre for galleries and studios in the vicinity of Colston Street. Stanfords map and travel bookshop on Corn Street discerningly stocks the Canal Companions. Sustrans have a shop at their offices on Cathedral Square, College Green.

Things to Do

TOURIST INFORMATION CENTRE - The Galleries. Tel: 0117 239 7685. BS1 3XD

BRISTOL FERRY BOAT CO - Tel: 0117 927 3416. Commendably frequent services make the ferries an ideal way of seeing much of the Floating Harbour if you haven't brought your own boat with you. Avon Gorge and river trips on selected dates.

CLIFTON SUSPENSION BRIDGE - Sion Place. Tel: 0117 974 4664. Brunel's wonderful bridge took thirty years from conception to completion, delayed by financial problems, social riots and indecision. All this and more surfaces from a trip to the visitor centre before going to see the bridge itself. BS8 3PA

SS GREAT BRITAIN - Great Western Dockyard. Tel: 0117 926 0680. Brunel's second great ocean liner launched in 1843. BS1 6TY

THE MATTHEW - Princes Wharf. Tel: 0117 927 6868. Working replica of John Cabot's *Matthew* in which he crossed the Atlantic and bumped into Newfoundland in 1497. BS1 4RN

M SHED - Princes Wharf, Wapping Road. Tel: 0117 352 6600. Bristol's social and industrial history atmospherically housed in a former dockyard transit shed. Admission free, closed Mons. BS1 4RN

AT-BRISTOL - Harbourside. Tel: 0117 915 1000. Multi-disciplined, 'hands on' visitor centre of special appeal to families. BS1 5LL

UNDERFALL YARD - Cumberland Road. Tel: 0117 929 3250. Fascinating visitor centre housed in harbour workshops/pump room. BS1 6XG

Connections

BUSES - First services X39 and 39 operate at frequent intervals to/from Bath via Keynsham and Saltford. Tel: 0871 200 2233.

TRAINS - Tel: 0345 748 4950. Major railhead. Useful local services via Keynsham to Bath and beyond.

Hanham   Map 2

CHEQUERS - riverside. Tel: 0117 329 1711. Two waterside pubs vie for your custom. This one was stylishly refurbished in 2014. BS15 3NU

OLD LOCK & WEIR - riverside. Tel: 0117 960 9345. Popular riverside pub featured in Conan Doyle's adventure *Micah Clark*. BS15 3NU

Keynsham   Map 2

Surely no child of the Sixties can ever think of Keynsham and not hear Horace Batchelor slowly ennunciating the way to spell it on Radio Luxembourg. St John's is an imposing parish church known for its Friday lunchtime recitals.

Eating & Drinking

LOCK KEEPER - by Keynsham Lock. Tel: 0117 986 2383. Canalside pub offering Young's and Bath ales, food, and a nice garden with petanque. BS31 2DD

Shopping

Plenty of shops and banks etc in the town centre less than ten minutes walk from the Avon via the railway station.

Connections

TRAINS - Useful local services to Bath and Bristol. Tel: 0345 748 4950.

Saltford   Map 3

Snug village of quiet by-roads away from the A4. The Manor house is of Norman origin. Handel is said to have been rhythmically inspired by the hammers in Saltford Brass Mill; but then, who wouldn't be!

Eating & Drinking

JOLLY SAILOR - by Saltford Lock. Tel: 01225 873002. Popular waterside inn offering a wide menu with the emphasis on seafood. BS31 3ER

BIRD IN HAND - High Street. Tel: 01225 873335. Well worth the stroll up from the river for a game of petanque in the garden overlooking the Bristol-Bath cycleway, but a convivial atmosphere inside and good food. Butcombe, Abbey ales etc. BS31 3EJ

Shopping

Useful (if not extensive) range of shops on A4 - pharmacy, Co-op, Tesco, newsagent, post office etc.

Things to Do

SALTFORD BRASS MILL - The Shallows. Tel: 0782 332 1768. Open 2nd and 4th Saturdays per month, 10am to 4pm, May-Oct. Lovingly restored brass mill featuring waterwheel and annealing furnace. BS31 3EY

Connections

BUSES - First services X39 and 39 operate at frequent intervals to/from Bath and Bristol Tel: 0871 200 2233.

SPRING tides occasionally lick their salty tongues up as far as Keynsham. But for the most part, other than after heavy rain, the Avon is pliant enough and the only boating hazards are the weirs which would draw the unwary away from the lock channels and the occasional knotty bend. In comparison to the Warwickshire Avon, this one is unsung; mistakenly considered a mere prelude or coda to the Kennet & Avon Canal proper whereas, in our opinion, it's a very pretty river in its own right; a joy to explore, on foot or afloat.

Scenically the landscape pivots on Hanham: to the east the valley is wide and water-meadowy; to the west wooded and gorge-like. Few buildings are foolhardy enough to encroach too closely upon the mercurial river, but here and there lies evidence of old industries which once needed to be near to the river because they relied upon it for transport: various light industries occupy premises - conspicuously dated 1881 - formerly used as a soap works; a weighbridge office remains at Londonderry Wharf where coal was once loaded on to barges; Hanham Colliery stood in what is now woodland on the north bank of the river downstream of the high A4174 road crossing. But arguably the most iconic industry (which must now be spoken of in the past tense) *was* the chocolate factory at Somerdale, closed in 2011 when production

was transferred to Poland. Looking not a little unlike a Lancashire textile mill - the sort of image that those who've explored the Leeds & Liverpool will be well familiar with - the works was built by Fry's in the 1920s and, at its busiest, employed five thousand people. There were only a few hundred left when the last Cadbury's Double Decker bar came off the production line, and the works has been turned into housing. On Keynsham Hams the beginning of the end for the Monmouth Rebellion took place in 1685 when the Duke of Beaufort's Cavalry routed the rebels prior to the bloody denouement at Sedgemoor. Bridge 211 is a substantial twin-arched structure. It carries the preserved Avon Valley Railway and the Bristol & Bath Railway Path across the river. The River Avon Trail changes banks at this point. Bitton, along with Kelston (Map 3), appears in Betjeman's campanological poem *Bristol*.

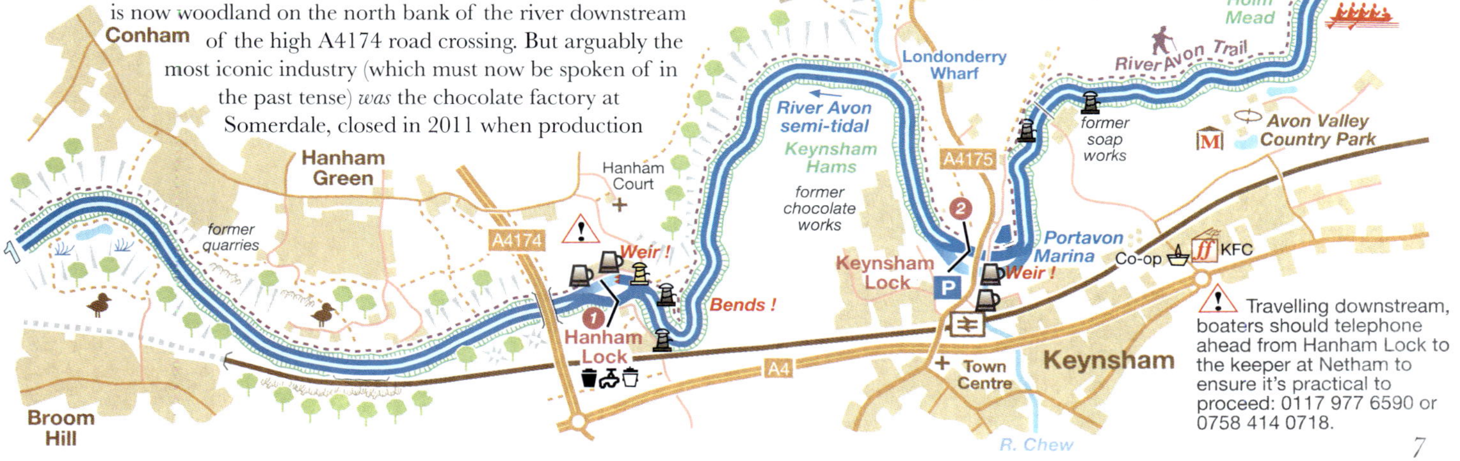

! Travelling downstream, boaters should telephone ahead from Hanham Lock to the keeper at Netham to ensure it's practical to proceed: 0117 977 6590 or 0758 414 0718.

3 RIVER AVON Swineford, Saltford and Newbridge 5mls/4lks/3hrs

SHARING its journey between Bristol and Bath with the A4 trunk road, Brunel's Great Western Railway, and the course of the rival Midland Railway, the River Avon meanders from lock to lock, encountering some of the most delicious countryside that North Somerset can muster. The Midland Railway has been reborn as the "Bristol & Bath Railway Path", one of the earliest Sustrans projects which have brought admirable new use to abandoned railways; though, nostalgically, one might be forgiven for day-dreaming that your boat be overtaken at any moment by the Pines Express puffing its way from Manchester to Bournemouth in the good old days of steam. Kelston station had no road access whatsoever and, according to an agreement with the local landowner who sanctioned its construction, was meant to remain open in perpetuity.

Whilst it's as a green lung for built-up Bristol and Bath that the Avon Valley is valued now, once it very much worked for its living, the manufacture of brass being a particular activity. The picturesque remains of a brass mill overlook Saltford Lock, but in the village itself one of the valley's mills, along with its furnace and waterwheel, has been painstakingly restored and opens its door to the general public on selected Saturdays.

Tree-topped Kelston Round Hill (or 'Tump') can be climbed from Kelston village and its summit is crossed by the Cotswold Way. From the top there are panoramic views south towards the Mendips and west to Wales. Kelston Park was built in 1770 for George III's physician, Sir Caesar Hawkins, the grounds being landscaped by Capability Brown. The house is now the headquarters of ARC; no, not the aggregates company, but the secular organisation founded by the late Duke of Edinburgh in 1995 to encourage alliances between religion and conservation.

The A4 elegantly crosses the river at New Bridge (208) erected in 1734. The railway bridges have less aesthetic value, but at least they provide pedestrians with the opportunity to cross the river in the regrettable absence of former ferries. Now noted for its Park & Ride, New Bridge was the western terminus of Bath's tramway system between 1904 and 1939.

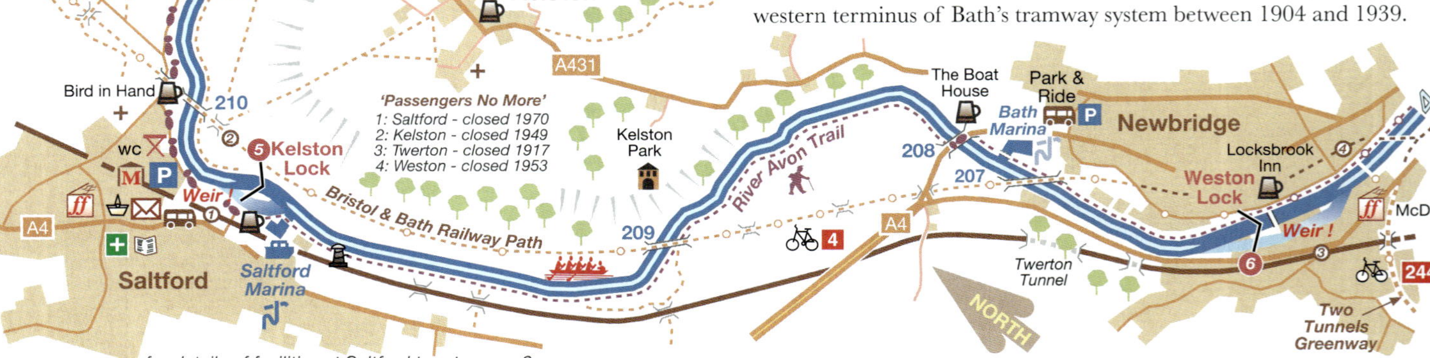

for details of facilities at Saltford turn to page 6

THE beautiful city of Bath plays host to the meeting of the Avon Navigation and the Kennet & Avon Canal. Arguably, only York and Chester, on the inland waterways, can muster such an appealing backdrop, so architecturally delicious a dessert with which to finish off a fine day's boating. Morning, may bring, however be warned, a reluctance to cast off from your moorings, for there is so much to be seen and to be done that the canal's implicit siren call will need to be balanced against the city's inherent attractions.

The Avon is actually navigable for a short distance upstream of the canal's junction with the river at the tail of Bath Bottom (or Widcombe) Lock. It is a detour well worth making (even if, due to 'safety issues', you are no longer permitted to moor) to get a close up view of the exquisite Pulteney Bridge.

Mooring points within the city limits can be found on the river, west of Churchill Road Bridge (198) in a setting overlooked by some handsome warehouses, or on the canal above Bath Top Lock from which there are panoramic views across this effulgent stone-built city.

The pedestrian, on the other hand, need only emerge from Bath Spa railway station (for no Pearson aficionado would be crass enough to come by car!) to find his or her way onto the towpath via Halfpenny

continued overleaf:

Locks
7 Bath Bottom Lock
8/9 Bath Deep Lock
10 Wash House Lock
11 Abbey View Lock
12 Pulteney Lock
13 Bath Top Lock

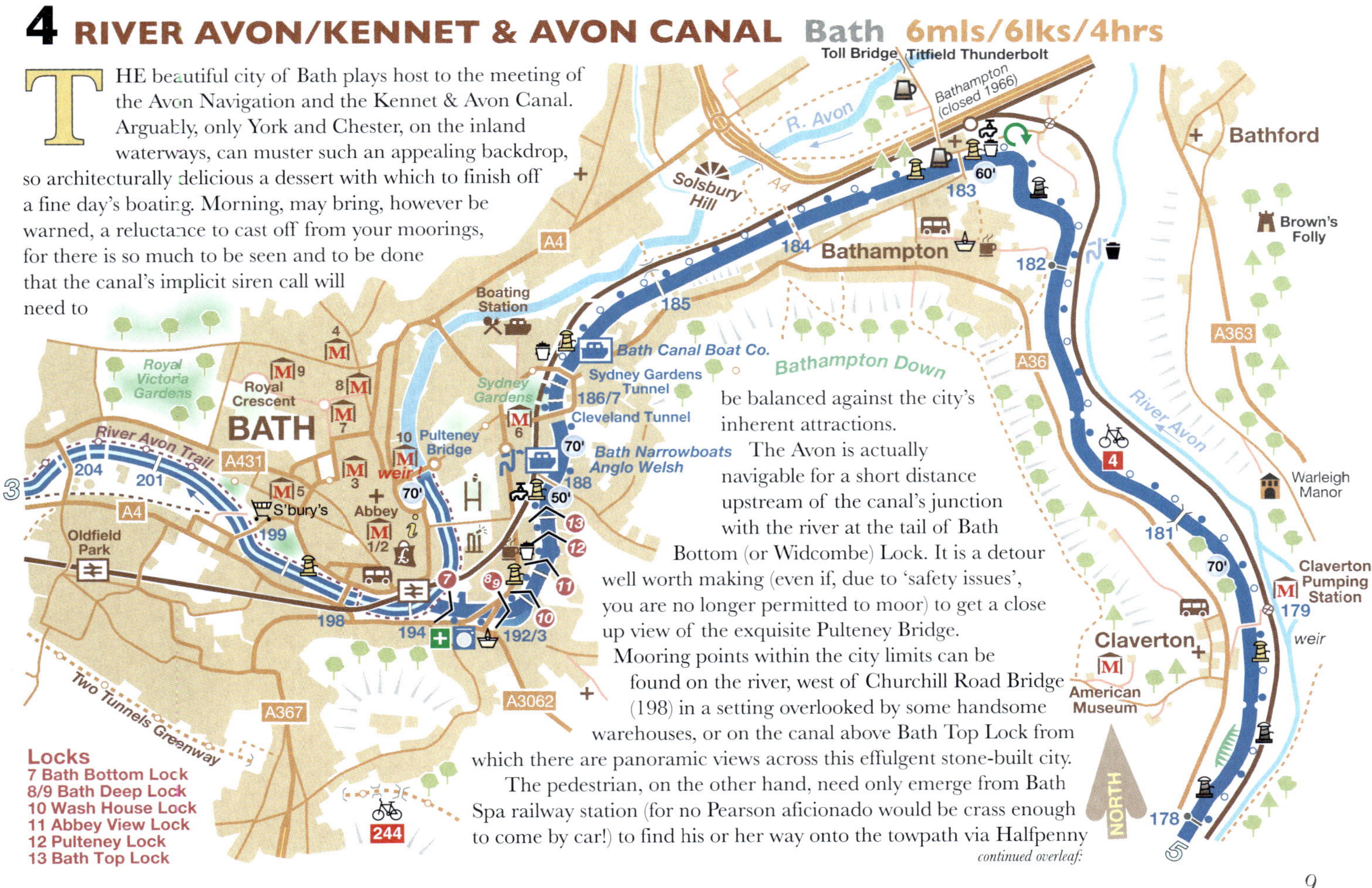

continued from page 9

Footbridge after which it's a simple heads or tails choice between exploring the river to the west or the canal to the east.

The River Avon

Redevelopment relentlessly redefines the 'Bristol' Avon's approach towards the centre of Bath. Crime writer, Andy Griffee, made use of this phenomenon in his second Johnson & Wilde mystery, *River Rats*. Apartment blocks and offices are recolonising the sites of Bath gas works and Stothert & Pitt's crane manufacturing works. Victoria Bridge (201), a suspension footbridge designed by James Dredge (see also Map 10), cocks an historic snook in the face of all the strident newcomers. Around the next bend come memories of one of Britain's best loved railways, the incomparable Somerset & Dorset system, which ran out of Bath's Green Park station across the Mendip Hills to Bournemouth. This gracious terminus, whose booking hall might easily be mistaken for an elegant town house, witnessed its last trains depart in a flurry of steam in 1966, but has survived more or less intact to become part of an indoor market and a Sainsbury's supermarket - one does not know whether to smile or weep.

Stothert & Pitt also had premises at Newark Works, which has become 'a creative hub for businesses'. Bath Quays footbridge opened in 2021. Some handsome former warehouses line the south bank of the river. You may moor opposite (though railings, erected for the safety of pedestrians, create something of an obstacle) and imagine you've arrived with a cargo of grain ex Avonmouth. Churchill Bridge (196) is a rather bland modern replacement for Bath Old Bridge, an attractive three-arched structure of mid eighteenth century origin. Then Brunel's Great Western Railway makes its first of two crossings of the river. Halfpenny Footbridge (194) tragically collapsed in 1877, overloaded by crowds on their way to the Bath & West Show, considerable loss of life ensued.

The Kennet & Avon Canal egresses to starboard (to the right, facing upstream) as the river curves northwards beneath the railway again. Boaters may explore upstream as far as Pulteney Bridge, though they must turn below the weir, and there are no opportunities to moor. The river wends its way past Bath Rugby Club's well known Recreation Ground on one bank and the elegant Parade Gardens on the other, one of the inland waterway system's most visual treats. Trip boats ply the picturesque reach above the weir upstream as far as Bathampton. Whilst, at Bath Boat Station, half a mile or so upstream, punts and skiffs may be hired for halcyon dalliances with one's current inamorata.

The Kennet & Avon Canal

Bath Bottom Lock is numbered 7th in the sequence from Bristol. Numbers 8 and 9 were combined when the canal was restored at this point in 1976. The new chamber has an intimidating depth of 19ft 5ins and fills from the sides. Succeeding locks ascend the hillside in a most agreeable manner, two of them sport ornamental iron footbridges at their tails, cast locally by Stothert & Pitt in their riverside foundry circa 1785 and painstakingly refurbished in 2011. Abbey View Lock fulfils its obligations and lock-wheelers may make the most of the view. Alongside is a former pump house chimney dating from 1840; there to be admired, perhaps, whilst indulging in home-made cakes or ice cream from the adjacent Pumpshed kiosk.

Bath Top Lock marks the beginning of a lengthy pound which would be half as long again were it not for the solitary lock at Bradford, ten miles away.* A useful boatyard and hire base follows before the canal romantically skirts the periphery of Sydney Gardens, encountering two tunnels and two elegant iron footbridges dated 1800. Cleveland House Tunnel is 173 feet long and the towpath runs through it. Above stands Cleveland House, former headquarters of the Kennet & Avon Canal Company. A trap-door in the tunnel roof was employed for facilitating the exchange of paperwork between clerks above and bargees below.

 *Don't, however, put your windlass too far out of reach, for you may need it to unlock the security bolts at swing-bridges 182 and 178.

Sydney Gardens were opened as a 'resort of pleasure' in 1795, they were provided with an hotel, a bowling green and a labyrinth. The canal builders had to pay handsomely to invade the gardens' serenity. Thirty years later that calm was disturbed again by the passage of the London to Bristol railway. At 165 yards, Sydney Gardens Tunnel is slightly shorter than its neighbour. Emerging from its eastern portal the canal runs shelf-like above the Avon Valley, shaking off the suburbs and sensing open countryside. Bridge 185 is a footbridge which replaced a swingbridge called Folly after a nearby pub was destroyed during a Second World War bombing raid. There are views, to the north-east, of Solsbury Hill, the inspiration behind Peter Gabriel's hit song of 1977. The little point on the summit is a triangulation pillar, 618 feet above sea level.

Essaying the easiest route around the hem of Bathampton Down, the canal continues to keep company with the River Avon, journeying on an almost north-south axis between Bathampton itself and Claverton. The scenery is delicious, and decidedly 'West Country' in feel, not something the canal network is necessarily well-acquainted with. There are views eastwards and upwards to Brown's Folly, a hillside tower constructed to provide employment following the Napoleonic Wars. Claverton Pumping Station was built to bring water up from the Avon to fill the canal. It was the work of John Rennie and its two water-wheels first began operating in 1813. It worked manfully for barely less than a century and a half before being replaced by a diesel pump. In 1976, however, it was lovingly restored by the Kennet & Avon Canal Trust. Whilst electric pumps do most of the work nowadays, the water-wheels perform their ancient rites on special days to an admiring public.

Bath Map 4

One doesn't need Unesco's 'World Heritage Site' seal of approval to facilitate the savouring of Bath's cohesive loveliness. By any criteria, this is one of Europe's most beautiful cities, and since one hasn't been able for over fifty years to arrive by steam train at the Queen Square (latterly Green Park) terminus of the Midland Railway, the Kennet & Avon Canal offers a consolatory alternative for visitors whose senses are fine-tuned to the more lofty ramifications of travel. The Roman Baths illustrate how far Bath's civilisation goes back, but it was the 18th century Welshman Beau Nash who galvanised the city's fame as a watering hole with few rivals. As Master of Ceremonies, he was the Tourism Development Officer of his era, and his grasp of publicity brought Society's crowds flocking to Bath as much for the social scene as for the quality of the waters. If Nash was Bath's best publicist, the architects John Wood, father and son, were the men most responsible for the city's inherent beauty and there is no way you should leave before inspecting the extraordinary Royal Crescent, the Pump Room, or Pulteney Bridge, let alone the 15th century Abbey and the Baths themselves. Make the most of it!

Eating & Drinking

BATHWICK BOATMAN - Bathwick. Tel: 01225 428844 Elegant boathouse restaurant on the isolated yet navigable reach of the Avon between Pulteney Weir and Bathampton Weir. BA2 6QE

CHEZ DOMINIQUE - Argyle Street. Tel: 01225 463482. French dining near Pulteney Bridge. BA2 4BQ

GRAZE - Brunel Square. Tel: 01225 429392. Bar, brewery and chop house by the station. BA1 1SX

GREEN PARK BRASSERIE - Tel: 01225 338565. Restaurant, bar and cafe housed in former station building. Open from 10.30am Tue-Sat. Eat heartily then catch the ghost train to Evercreech Junction or wait for the live jazz Wed-Sat evenings. BA1 1JB

HOP POLE - Upper Bristol Road. Tel: 01225 446327. Bath Ales pub easily accessed from towpath at Bridge 201. BA1 3AR

LOCKSBROOK INN - Locksbrook Road. Tel: 01225 427119. Gastropub (formerly known as The Dolphin) adjacent Weston Lock (Map 3). BA1 3EN

OLD GREEN TREE - Green Street. Tel: 01225 448259. RCH from Somerset and Wickwar from Gloucestershire are regulars on tap in this wonderful *GBG* listed time-warp of a pub. Lunches. BA1 2JZ

THE PUMP SHED - Lock 11. Home made cakes for hungry lock-wheelers etc.

THE RAVEN - Queen Street. Tel: 01225 425045. Lively, refurbished real ale pub which features in the *Good Beer Guide*. Famed for its generous pies 'constructed' from local ingredients! BA1 1HE

SALLY LUNN'S - North Parade Passage. Tel: 01225 461634. A Bath institution which charmingly contrives to transcend its tourist status as the city's oldest house and the home of the world famous Bath Bun. Tea room and restaurant facilities. BA1 1NX

SEAFOODS - Kingsmead Square. Tel: 01225 465190. Award-winning eat-in or take-away fish & chips. BA1 2AA

continued overleaf:

continued from page 11:

Shopping

Avoid the city centre chain stores and you'll be well rewarded. The Guildhall Market is a good starting point, it's located between the High Street and Pulteney Bridge. Green Park Market is housed in the gracious environment of the old Midland Railway terminus: Farmers' Market on Saturdays; Artisans Market 2nd Sundays; Vintage Market 1st and last Sundays. It is practical to moor nearby on the Avon and stock up the galley at Sainsbury's, but Bath's handsome thoroughfares are filled with independent retailers, and it's much more fun to seek them out. Bibliophile's will be in their element: Whiteman's may be mourned, but Topping's excellent bookshop is on The Paragon (Tel: 01225 428111 - BA1 5LS); George Bayntun's antiquarian bookshop, print gallery and book-binding specialist is on Manvers Street (Tel: 01225 446000 - BA1 1JW) near the railway station; and Persephone Books (specialists in 20th century women writers) have recently moved into 8 Edgar Buildings on George Street (Tel: 01225 425050 - BA1 2EE). At the top of the canal locks there's a handy Tesco Express overlooking Bridge 188.

Things To Do

TOURIST INFORMATION CENTRE - Terrace Walk. Tel: 01225 614420. BA1 1LN
CITY SIGHTSEEING - open top bus tours of Bath and its environs.
THE ROMAN BATHS & PUMP ROOM (1) - Abbey Churchyard. Tel: 01225 477785. BA1 1LZ
THERMAE BATH SPA (2) - Hot Bath Street. Tel: 01225 331234. Thermal baths and steam rooms including spectacular rooftop pool. BA1 1SJ
JANE AUSTEN CENTRE (3) - Gay Street. Tel: 01225 443000. Bath was the setting for *Northanger Abbey* and *Persuasion* and their authoress lived in the city from 1801 to 1806. BA1 2NT

MUSEUM OF BATH AT WORK (4) - Julian Road. Tel: 01225 318348. Antidote to Bath's (understandable) tendency to 18th century overkill. BA1 2RH
HERSCHEL MUSEUM OF ASTRONOMY (5) - New King Street. Tel: 01225 446865. Small museum in former home of famous astronomer. BA1 2BL
HOLBURNE MUSEUM (6) - Tel: 01225 388569. Glorious art gallery located by Sydney Gardens within easy reach of the canal. Shop/cafe. BA2 4DB
FASHION MUSEUM (7) - Assembly Rooms. Tel: 01225 477789. Dress & garb down the ages. BA1 2QH
BUILDING OF BATH (8) - Paragon. Tel: 01225 333895. The city's architectural history. BA1 5NA
No.1 ROYAL CRESCENT (9) - Tel: 01225 428126. An inside peep at a Palladian masterpiece. BA1 2LR
VICTORIA ART GALLERY (10) - Bridge Street. Tel: 01225 477233. Locally inspired art. BA2 4AT

Connections

BUSES - services throughout the area from the riverside bus station. For an enjoyable excursion leap aboard service 172 which runs through Radstock (which has an excellent museum) to the cathedral city of Wells. Tel: 0871 200 2233.
TRAINS - Tel: 0345 748 4950. Frequent Great Western Railway services to/from London Paddington plus useful local links with Bradford-on-Avon, Keynsham and Bristol for towpath walkers and cyclists.
TAXIS - Abbey Cars. Tel: 01225 444444.
BATH BIKE HIRE - Sydney Wharf (Bridge 188). Tel: 01225 447276. BA2 4EL

Bathampton   Map 4

Bathampton was, until 1983, the site of Harbutt's Plasticine factory, something that generations of children had been thankful for since William Harbutt invented the substance in 1897. The canalside church will be of interest to Australian boating parties for the first Governor of New South Wales lies buried here, and it features a small Australian Chapel. Bathampton (aka Batheaston) Toll Bridge dates from 1872, though an earlier structure replaced a ferry circa 1850. Cars cost a pound, pedestrians gratis.

Eating & Drinking

THE GEORGE INN - Mill Lane (canalside Bridge 183). Tel: 01225 425079. Chef & Brewer inn predating the canal and said to be haunted by the loser of the last legally fought duel in England. BA2 6TR
BATHAMPTON MILL - riverside (down from Bridge 183). Pub/restaurant. Tel: 01225 469758. BA2 6TS

Shopping

Convenience store to south of canal. Railway enthusiasts won't want to eschew the opportunity to visit Simon Castens' excellent Titfield Thunderbolt bookshop on the far side of the Toll Bridge (Tel: 01225 462332 - BA1 7DE), though it's usually only open on Thursdays, so wise to phone ahead and check to avoid disappointment. HQ of Wild Swan Books too!

Connections

BUSES - services 12/265 operate to/from Bath city centre. Tel: 0871 200 2233.

Claverton   Map 4

CLAVERTON PUMPING STATION - adjacent Bridge 179 (walk down Ferry Lane and over the railway level crossing). Tel: 01225 483001. Idyllically located on the Avon and generally open last Saturday of the month. On no account should this be missed if at all possible! BA2 7BH
AMERICAN MUSEUM - Claverton Manor. Tel: 01225 460503. Substantial early 19th century mansion housing fascinating displays of Americana. Light refreshments available. Open Easter to October afternoons but not usually Mondays except during August and Bank Holidays. 20 mins walk uphill from Br. 179. BA2 7BD

ACCEPTING its cue from the Avon with aplomb, the canal winds enchantingly through the steeply wooded valley, becoming so enraptured of the river that it straddles it ecstatically, not once but twice. Completed in 1805 and 1798 respectively, Rennie's Dundas and Avoncliff aqueducts are imbued with the graciousness of the Georgian era so inviolately that, when the railway was built in the middle of the succeeding century, the additional arch at each location endeavoured to meld seamlessly with its elegant progenitor; imitation being the sincerest form of flattery.

Progressing by boat (necessarily at a snail's pace on account of a plethora of residential craft moored bow to stern from Bath to Bradford), on foot or by bicycle (for this is Sustrans National Cycle Route 4) the large numbers of explorers who savour this peerless stretch of canal have reason to be grateful to the stalwarts who campaigned so effectively for the re-opening of the Kennet & Avon Canal in 1990: truly, the Avon Valley would seem bereft without it now. Indeed, so lovely are the surroundings, that it is easy to overlook the fact that the canal was built, not as a lofty means for facilitating the admiration of scenery, but for the altogether more mundane purpose of carrying goods. In this regard it was initially hugely successful, boosted here by traffic off the Somersetshire Coal Canal with which a junction was formed at Dundas Aqueduct.

To discover more about the colourful

continued overleaf:

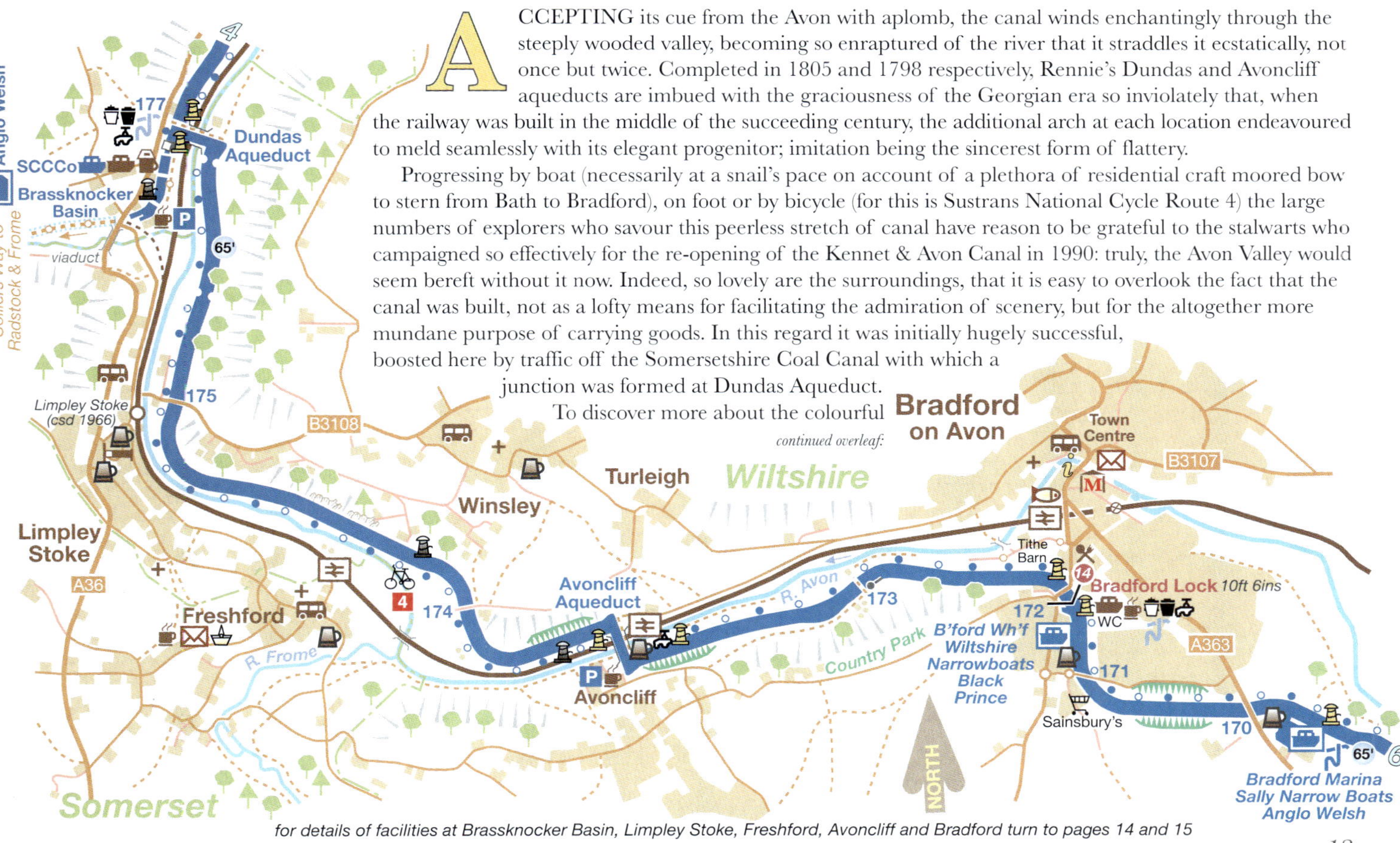

for details of facilities at Brassknocker Basin, Limpley Stoke, Freshford, Avoncliff and Bradford turn to pages 14 and 15

continued from page 13:

history of the Coal Canal, visit Brassknocker Basin where a reconstituted SCCCo. display an illustrated history of the concern on a sequence of interpretive panels housed in a small, informal visitor centre. Incidentally, sections of the Coal Canal, later transformed into railways, have survived to become public foot and cycle paths such as the Colliers Way.

But it's the K&A which largely concerns us here, exchanging Somerset for Wiltshire at the same time as it crosses Dundas Aqueduct, named after Charles Dundas, the first chairman of the Kennet & Avon Canal Company: some epitaph, some immortality! If you expected boating to be confined to the canal, it will come as something of a surprise to see rowers being put through their paces on the river below. So prone to leakage was the section between Limpley Stoke and Avoncliff, that when the canal was restored it was with a layer of hardcore on a porous membrane, which is itself covered by a second layer of polythene sheeting and a final bed of reinforced concrete. From time to time the canal narrows at points where stop planks can be inserted in the event of a breach. Avoncliff echoes Dundas in the canal's right-angled crossing of the river: though, like a catchy hook in a memorable pop song, there's nothing staid or repetitive about so delightful an encore.

Delving through the woodlands and meadows of a popular Country Park (where the British Museum stored valuables in former quarry workings during WWII) the K&A reaches Bradford-on-Avon where the first sod was cut just outside the Canal Tavern in 1794. A pack-horse bridge and canalside medieval tithe barn remind us that at two centuries and a bit old the canal is merely a johnny-come-lately. There were once two wharves in this thriving wool town. Upper Wharf is especially attractive with dry dock, wharfinger's house and a K&A Canal Trust shop.

Negotiating a lengthy cutting which more or less successfully masks the suburban fringes of Bradford, the canal passes beneath the Trowbridge road before encountering a busy marina. Then, accompanied by woodland bordering the Avon, it heads eastwards along a five mile pound which extends to Semington.

Brassknocker Basin — Map 5

More properly Monkton Combe, but the village lies a mile to the west of the canal whose focus is on an imaginative modern development near the junction of the erstwhile Somersetshire Coal Canal. The Colliers Way recreational path follows the old canal/railway and links up with the Two Tunnels Greenway (see Map 4) to create a circular, traffic-free route of exceptional interest and beauty.

Eating & Drinking
ANGELFISH - Brassknocker Basin. Tel: 01225 723483. Cafe and licensed restaurant. 10am-6pm. BA2 7JD

Shopping
Spar convenience store in garage on main road.

Things to Do
BATH NARROWBOATS - Brassknocker Basin. Tel: 01225 447276. Electric day boat, Canadian canoe and bicycle hire. BA2 7JD

Limpley Stoke — Map 5

Long-winded village on the A36 Bath-Southampton road which crosses Midford Brook on a handsome example of one of the earliest road viaducts. The old railway station (now a private home) still retaining its GWR nameboard, is visible from the canal. The Camerton branch ran from here (over the bed of the Somersetshire Coal Canal) until the early 1950s. The much loved Ealing comedy *The Titfield Thunderbolt* was filmed on the line after it had been officially closed. Bus 265 operates half-hourly (hourly Sun) from stops near bridges 175/177 to/from Bath and Trowbridge.

Freshford — Map 5

Delectable stone village across the Avon from the canal but accessible on foot (or by train) from Avoncliff. Community shop (PO Tue & Fri am) and cafe (Tel: 01225 723249) and eponymous inn (Tel: 01225 722250) beside the Frome offering Box Steam Brewery ales.

Avoncliff — Map 5

The impressive block of buildings west of the aqueduct were orginally weavers' houses, then a workhouse, then a WWI convalescent home, then a hotel, and now houses once more. Spare a moment to look at the tiny railway station, almost as pretty and as cared for as if it were on some preserved steam line.

Eating & Drinking
CROSS GUNS - Tel: 01225 862335. Popular hostelry which predates the canal. Tables spill down to decking beside the river offering a great view of the aqueduct. Beers from Box Steam Brewery. Great for cider too. Food available all day every day. BA15 2HB
Try also: No. 10 Tea Gardens (Fri-Sun) beside aqueduct.

Connections
TRAINS - decent service daily to/from Bradford and Bath very handy for towpath walks. Also affords easy pedestrian access to Freshford. Tel: 0345 748 4950.

Bradford-on-Avon   Map 5

Teetering on the brink of its clifftop setting, mellow, medieval Bradford-on-Avon resembles a petite version of Bath, and being smaller can be appreciated and assimilated all the more easily. Its architecture appears capable of absorbing sunlight and then emitting it like storage heaters. Amongst many outstanding buildings you'll come upon a Saxon church, a tithe barn and a 14th century bridge with a chapel on it. One of an exclusive club of four remaining in England, regular *Canal Companion* users will easily be able to run through the locations of the other three, all linked to the inland waterways. Bradford's fortunes were built on wool and weaving and many of its buildings, both domestic and commercial, reflect the heyday of this lost industry; solely the relentless tide of traffic being able to deflect from the town's inherent beauty.

Eating & Drinking

BRIDGE TEA ROOMS - Bridge Street. Tel: 01225 865537. Charmingly old-fashioned tea room across the street from Bradford's lovely bridge. BA15 1BY
CANAL TAVERN - Frome Road (canalside below Bradford Lock). Tel: 01225 866100. Wadworth ales and a wide range of food. BA15 1LE
HARLEES - Frome Road (adjacent railway station). Tel: 01225 865252. Fish & chips. BA15 1LA
K&A TRUST TEA ROOM - canalside above Bradford Lock. Tel: 01225 863683. Cafe and canalia. BA15 1LE
LOCK INN - canalside below Bradford Lock. Tel: 01225 727668. Lively establishment offering food (famed for its Boatman's Breakfasts) real ale and an infectious sense of humour. Canoe hire. BA15 1LE
THE MAHARAJA - adjacent canal wharf. Tel: 01225 866424. Tandoori restaurant/take-away. BA15 1LE
RAVELLO - St Margaret's Street. Tel: 01225 781666. Italian restaurant. BA15 1DA

THAI BARN - St Margaret's Street. Tel: 01225 866443. Award-winning Thai restaurant. BA15 1DA
THE WEAVING SHED - Kingston Mills. Tel: 01225 866519. Contemporary riverside eatery. BA15 1EJ

Shopping

The town centre is less than ten minutes walk down from the canal and there are heaps of nice old-fashioned shops, as exemplified by Brown's Hardware on Silver Street. A small bookshop called Ex Libris: new at the front, secondhand out the back. Interesting array of outlets at the Tithe Barn Workshops & Galleries. More prosaically, there's a Co-op supermarket (with post office counter) housed in a former mill building by the river bridge and a larger Sainsbury's supermarket close to Bridge 171.

Things to Do

TOURIST INFORMATION - St Margaret's Street Tel: 01225 865797. BA15 1DE
BRADFORD MUSEUM - Bridge Street. Well displayed local history above library. Admission free. BA15 1BY
TT CYCLES - Elm Cross Business Park. Tel: 01225 867187. Bike hire, sales, repairs eetc. BA15 1LE

Connections

TRAINS - Bradford's Brunellian station provides frequent connections for Bath & Bristol via Avoncliff and Westbury via Trowbridge. Tel: 0345 748 4950.
TAXIS - Bradford-on-Avon Cars. Tel: 01225 862277.

Trowbridge   Map 6

Boaters on a finite holiday and walkers with Devizes or Bradford in their sights can blithely pass by Wiltshire's unlikely county town, but - even now shorn of Bowyers pie factory and Ushers brewery - we find it an enjoyable place to visit with a wealth of fine architecture.

Eating & Drinking

Fast food outlets by Bridge 167: Chinese (Tel: 01225 766788); and fish & chips/roasts (Tel: 0778 308 8219).

Shopping

Full range of shops and banks in the town centre. Interesting indoor market. Lidl supermarket about ten minutes walk from Hilperton Wharf. Convenience store to west of Bridge 167. The petrol station near Bridge 166 has a post office counter and cash machine.

Connections

BUSES - serice 68 operates to/from Trowbridge Mon-Sat from stop by Br. 167. Stagecoach service 49 links Trowbridge with Devizes. Tel: 0871 200 2233.
TRAINS - to/from Bath via Bradford. Tel: 0345 748 4950.
TAXIS - Alpha. Tel: 01225 753218.

Semington   Map 6

SOMERSET ARMS - 5 minutes walk south of Bridge 160. Tel: 01380 870067. *Good Beer Guide* listed 'coaching inn' providing accommodation, locally brewed real ales and lunch and dinner daily (12-8 Sun). BA14 6JR

Seend Cleeve   Map 7

THE BARGE INN - canalside Bridge 154. Tel: 01380 828230. Nice pub, idyllically located canalside. Wadworth beer and a wide range of food. SN12 6QB
BREWERY INN - 5 minutes south from Bridge 154. Tel: 01380 828463. Unspoilt village local. SN12 6PX

Seend   Map 7

Formerly a prosperous centre for weaving - witness some fine Georgian houses of golden stone - though nowadays the effect is somewhat compromised by traffic on the A361. Post office stores.

Sells Green   Map 7

THREE MAGPIES - north of Bridge 149. Tel: 01380 828389. Wadworths, bar and restaurant meals. Camping and caravanning facilities. SN12 6RN

SELDOM far from sight and mind between Bath and Bradford, the River Avon turns northwards towards its source in the Cotswold hills west of Malmesbury. Henceforth bereft of riverine companionship until it bumps into the Kennet at Hungerford, the canal skirts the urban periphery of Trowbridge. Corrugated clad warehouses invoke little incentive to deepen the acquaintance, but their blandness is misleading, for the county town repays exploration by those with time at their disposal. An Act was passed in 1769 to build a branch into the town but construction didn't ensue. Two modest, yet elegant aqueducts transport the canal over the River Biss, a tributary of the Avon, and the Westbury-Bath railway line respectively. The single arched Biss Aqueduct, whilst never soaring to the same heights (literally or metaphorically) as Dundas and Avoncliff further west, is especially handsome. And then there are the remains - admittedly scant - of two wharves beside Hilperton Road Bridge, Marsh Wharf and Hilperton Wharf both being built to serve Trowbridge in the absence of that branch. To the north the Shredded Wheat factory at Staverton is a prominent landmark - when the poet Edward Thomas bicycled past it in 1913, sourcing copy for *In Pursuit of Spring*, the mill was operating under the auspices of the Phoenix Swiss Milk Company.

It is difficult to visualise sleepy Semington as a busy canal junction but such was the case in the early part of the 19th Century. The Wilts & Berks Canal, opened in 1810, ran from here for fifty heavily locked miles to the Thames at Abingdon (see Map 24) via Melksham, Swindon and Challow. Hampered, perhaps, by being a narrow-beam canal between broad-beam arteries, its commercial success was short-lived, competition from the GWR between London and Bristol bringing about its downfall; the first proposal for its abandonment came as early as 1874. Through traffic became impossible following the collapse of an aqueduct between Chippenham and Calne in 1901 and the canal was formally closed at the beginning of the First World War. Little evidence of the junction remains, except for the toll collector's house - now advertising B&B. The Wilts & Berks Canal Trust are ambitiously campaigning to restore the canal to full navigation, and the Duchess of Cornwall symbolically cut the first sod of the revitalised canal's proposed new course in 2010.

The two locks at Semington mark the end of a five mile level pound from Bradford-on-Avon, and they are quickly followed by a flight of five at Seend. An aqueduct carries the canal across the A350.

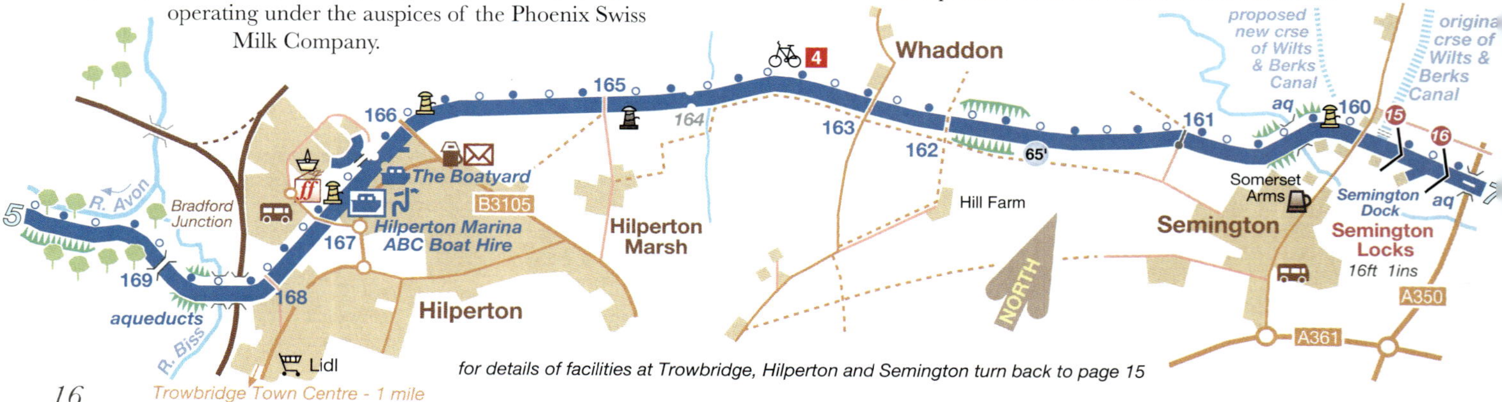

for details of facilities at Trowbridge, Hilperton and Semington turn back to page 15

LUSH and larksong-filled, the countryside around Seend Cleeve is utterly disarming; southwards, throughout this length of the canal, there are views towards the high, bare ridge of Salisbury Plain. In Spring celandine lines the banks like a yellow woven pattern in a green scarf. Swing bridges (for which you may need a windlass to loosen the security bolts) abound, and there's a flight of five locks too, giving you extra time to appreciate the soft rolling hills that characterise this part of Wiltshire.

Amongst the picturesque group of buildings adjoining swing-bridge 156 is Littleton Mill. In 1802 it was a cloth mill and the scene of an orgy of loom breaking as locals attempted (hopelessly, in hindsight) to stem the remorseless march of technological advance. One of the rioters, a 19 year old called Thomas Helliker, was hung for his trouble, and lies entombed in the churchyard of St James, Trowbridge.

A modern pump beside Lock 17 recycles water to the top of the flight. The Barge Inn, situated below the middle lock of the five, is one of the most popular pubs at this end of the K&A and stands on the site of Seend Wharf. Dating back to 1805, in 1916 it became the home of the 'Wiltshire Giant' Fred Kempster (8 feet 2 inches) whose brother-in-law was the landlord.

A field to the east of The Barge was the site of industry in the nineteenth century, ironstone having been discovered on Seend Hill. Three blast furnaces were built, together with tramway connections to the canal and a broad gauge branch to the Devizes railway line, but the enterprise proved financially unsound. Nevertheless, mining of iron ore continued sporadically right through to the Second World War. The lines of the two tramways are still discernible, whilst the positively baronial house of the iron master (who could obviously lay claim to a classical education, for he called it Ferrum Lodge*) is visible on the hillside above Lock 19.

Boaters congregate overnight between bridges 149 and 152. The countryside is blissful and paths radiate from the swing-bridges for the exercising of dogs. In doing so one might come upon the melancholy trackbed of an old railway which once linked Devizes with the outside world. Later, as the light fades, the campanologists of Seend may lull you to sleep amidst the occasional clatter of ghost trains.

Bridge 148 marks the site of Wragg's Wharf from which a family of that name once plied with a pair of boats to and from Dunkerton Colliery on the Somerset Coal Canal. The canal drifts across Summerham Brook on a small aqueduct. Ever mindful of maximising water supply, the K&A utilises water from the brook which is channelled into the waterway via the Seend Feeder.

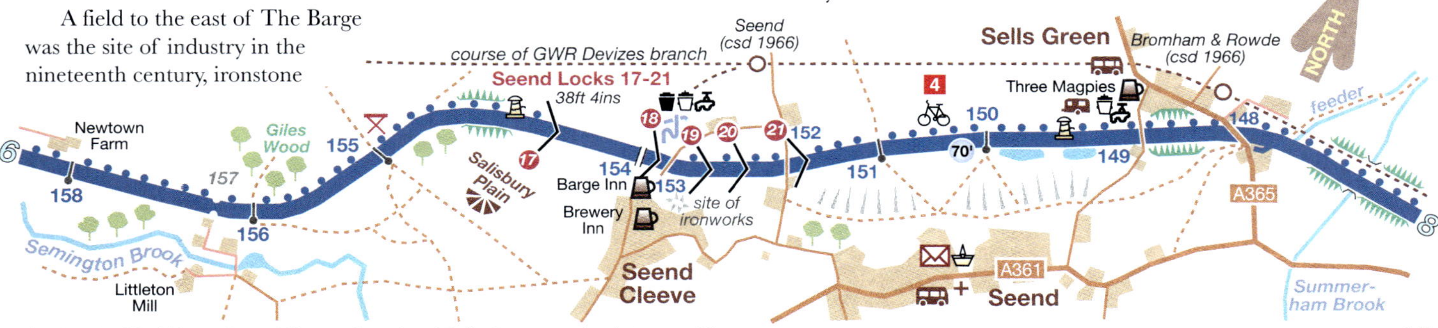

for details of facilities at Seend Cleeve, Seend and Sells Green turn back to page 15

*though now it is known as 'Ferrum House'

RENNIE'S spectacular set of sixteen locks and side ponds, completed in 1810, was the last major engineering work to be completed before the canal's opening, and, equally significantly, one of the final restoration projects to be finished prior to its reopening a hundred and eighty years later.

The locks exert a powerful influence on the waterway to this day, with cruising itineraries being carefully planned around their intimidating and/or exhilarating presence. One of Robert Aickman's 'Seven Wonders of the Waterways', the whole Devizes flight of 29 widebeam locks raises (or lowers) the level of the canal by 237 feet in just over two miles. They come in three groups: seven at Foxhangers, the acclaimed sixteen at Caen Hill and six at the town end of the flight; and all the chambers weigh in at a universal 8 feet and 2 inches rise/fall. Whilst the locks were under construction a tramroad provided a link between Foxhangers and Devizes, as evidenced by the wide towpath arches in the road bridges that cross the canal. The locks were built of brick, supplied by the now disused brickworks beside the Caen Hill section. To address serious water supply problems, a back pumping station

was installed at Foxhangers in 1996, capable of returning thirty-two million litres of water per day to the top of the flight - equivalent to one lockful every eleven minutes.

But how does it feel to arrive at the foot (or top) of the flight with all those locks ahead of you? Well you certainly won't be doing much else that day, five to six hours being considered a good performance for clearance of the flight. But don't be intimidated, for the locks are well maintained and relatively easy to operate, and, in high season at least, you'll probably have volunteer lock-keepers to assist you. Settle in to a rhythm, relax and enjoy every moment of one of the most defining experiences the canal network has to offer. The surroundings only add to your enjoyment, and there are some splendid views, notably in a north-easterly direction towards the chalk downlands, exemplified by Oliver's Castle, an Iron Age fort, pinpointed by five trees on its summit.

Bridge 142 is known as Prison Bridge. Between 1817 and 1920 it was overlooked by the Wiltshire County House of Correction, a polygon-shaped gaol. Over the years, several public hangings took place and barge trips advertised to attend the proceedings. In 1824

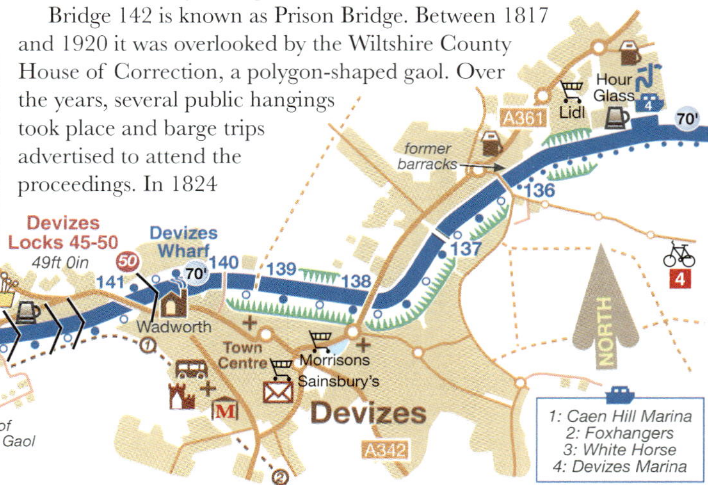

John Goodman and Edward Amor of Honeystreet Wharf (Map 10) were hung publically for theft and violent assault, whereas now they would probably get away with a stern warning.

Devizes once possessed three wharves, Sussex, Lower and Town, of which only the latter survives. Built around 1812, its early trade was in coal from the Somersetshire Coal Canal, later traffic bringing in agricultural goods, brick, stone and timber; plus, of course, raw materials and finished products heading to and from Wadworth's adjacent brewery.

Today two admirably restored buildings stand proudly on the wharf: a former warehouse now serves as the Wharf Theatre, whilst an erstwhile granary and wine store is now the headquarters of the Kennet & Avon Canal Trust. With a small hire fleet and trip boat also based here, the wharf buzzes with activity on summer weekends and, with two lengths of visitor moorings, is an excellent place to recuperate from (or gird your loins for) the rigours of Devizes Locks. Stick your head out of the boat as dawn breaks and you're apt to be greeted by a West Country 'marning'.

Devizes — Map 8

Blue plaques abound in this most architecturally stimulating of market towns, whilst in beer-drinking circles, it is widely known for the excellence of the ale brewed by Wadworth, from whose lofty red brick Victorian premises a horse and dray still makes local deliveries about the town. David Verey's 1956 *Shell Guide to Wiltshire* spoke enthusiastically of the 'restrained dignity of its streets, the red brick Georgian houses contrasting with ashlar-faced public buildings in the Bath manner and the fine proportions of its market place' and sixty years and more have failed to invalidate him. There are aspirations of turning Thomas Henry Wyatt's Grecian Assize Courts (near Bridge 141) into new accommodation for the Wiltshire Museum. The parish church of St John the Baptist, fully restored after a serious fire, repays a peep, especially if one of its 'sitters' is on hand to show you round. Ask to see the green man in the Norman nave! Yes, saddled with an, at best, intuitive street plan (seasoned by secret cobbled alleyways) Devizes is, to coin a phrase, full of surprizes.

Eating & Drinking

BEAR HOTEL - Market Place. Tel: 01380 722444. Reassuringly traditional hotel dating from 1599 offering morning coffees, bar lunches, afternoon teas, and evening meals. Wadworth's ambrosial ales. SN10 1HS
BLACK HORSE - Bath Road (by Bridge 142/Lock 47). Tel: 01380 723930. Wadworth pub with large canalside garden, moorings. SN10 2AU
BRITISH LION - Estcourt Street. Tel: 01380 720665. *GBG* listed real ale/cider lover's paradise. SN10 1LQ
CAEN HILL CAFE - canalside by Lock 44. Tel: 01380 724880. Charming setting for soups, sandwiches, home made cakes and ice creams. SN10 1QR
HOUR GLASS - Horton Avenue. Tel: 01380 727313. Newbuild Marston's bar/restaurant with canalside terrace adjoining Devizes Marina Village. Open from 10am daily. SN10 2RH
MAYFLOWER - St John's Street. Tel: 01380 720600. Oriental cuisine. Closed Sundays. SN10 1BD
VAULTS - St John's Street. Tel: 01380 721443. Micro-pub and beer shop belonging to Kennet & Avon Brewery - a name inspired by the canal. SN10 1BN

Shopping

Access from the Wharf to the town centre is via Couch Lane and Snuff Street, beyond which the Market Place opens up in all its glory: Thursday is the main Market Day but there is also a Farmers' Market on the first Saturday in the month. The Covered Market is a lovely building in its own right and operates virtually daily in one guise or another. Sainsbury's (post office counter) and Morrisons fight it out for your day to day needs. M&S Food Hall. Bookworms will enjoy Devizes Books, housed in the augustly classical setting of Handel House on Sidmouth Street; location additionally, of the excellent butcher, Walter Rose, established as 'recently' as 1847. Launderette at the west end of the Market Place.

Things to Do

CANAL TRUST CENTRE - Devizes Wharf. Tel: 01380 721279. Excellent shop, cafe and museum operated by the Kennet & Avon Canal Trust. SN10 1EB
WILTSHIRE MUSEUM - Long Street. Tel: 01380 727369. Rewarding museum, gallery and library owned by the Wiltshire Archaeological and Natural History Society. SN10 1NS
WADWORTH VISITOR CENTRE - New Park Street. Tel: 01380 723361. Self-guided, interactive journeys into this famously independent Wiltshire brewery's heritage and current brewing techniques. SN10 1JW

Connections

BUSES - Devizes' train services were Beechinged & Marples'd into a siding in 1966, so now one must rely on buses. Stagecoach service 49 links the town with railheads at Trowbridge and Swindon via Avebury offering an excursion to see the Stones. Faresaver X72 runs to/from Bath. Tel: 0871 200 2233. Local 'Connect 2' services 100 & 101 link Devizes with Pewsey - Tel: 01722 32615 to book a seat.
TAXIS - Devizes Taxis. Tel: 01380 723129.

9 KENNET & AVON CANAL The Cannings 5mls/0lks/2hrs

WERE one in search of some sort of English equivalent to 'La France Profonde', surely the Vale of Pewsey would fit the bill. But us Anglo-Saxons are as reticent when it comes to landscape as we are human relations, so a perfunctory 'the scenery's not bad' must suffice. Scudding clouds cast energetic shadows on the sculptured downs as the canal's dreamlike progress is punctuated by remote villages, for the most part now bereft of shops and, in several cases, pubs as well. Evidently, though, they have retained their churches, as exemplified by St Mary's at Bishop's Cannings whose spire, seen from a distance, soars against the edge of the downs like a miniature Salisbury. In these splayed out settlements, the widespread use of brick surprises, outnumbering stone and thatch until you see pockets of chalk exposed on the downs and realise that it would not be an ideal building material.

Solely the most time-constrained canal traveller will be able to resist a detour up on to the tumuli-littered top of the downs, scaling the chalky escarpment to where the Wansdyke once delineated prehistoric territories. These Marlborough Downs form the highest part of Wiltshire, just falling short of a thousand feet above sea level. From the canal's perspective you are reminded of the paintings of Eric Ravilious.

This is the Long Pound, and it lives up to its name, consisting of fifteen restful, lock-less miles with only the odd swing bridge to disturb a boater's reverie. Participants in the annual Eastertide Devizes to Westminster International Canoe Marathon are lulled into a misleadingly lock-less trance before the real business of portaging kicks in.

Summary of Facilities

The BRIDGE INN at Horton is the most popular with canallers by virtue of its location beside Bridge 134 (Tel: 01380 860273 - SN10 2JS), but there are also good village pubs in Bishop's Cannings and All Cannings; the CROWN INN (Tel: 01380 860218 - SN10 2JZ) and KINGS ARMS (Tel: 01380 860328 - SN10 3PA) respectively and, being in the heart of Wadworthshire, you know full well what beer they serve. The only shop for miles is at All Cannings, a charming establishment run by the community for the community - Tel: 01380 862913 SN10 3PA. The village's telephone kiosk has been turned into an informal bookstall. Stagecoach bus 49 provides Bishop's Cannings with a good service to/from Devizes and Swindon and there's a stop adjacent to Bridge 134. 'Connect 2' buses serve the other villages - see Pewsey page 23.

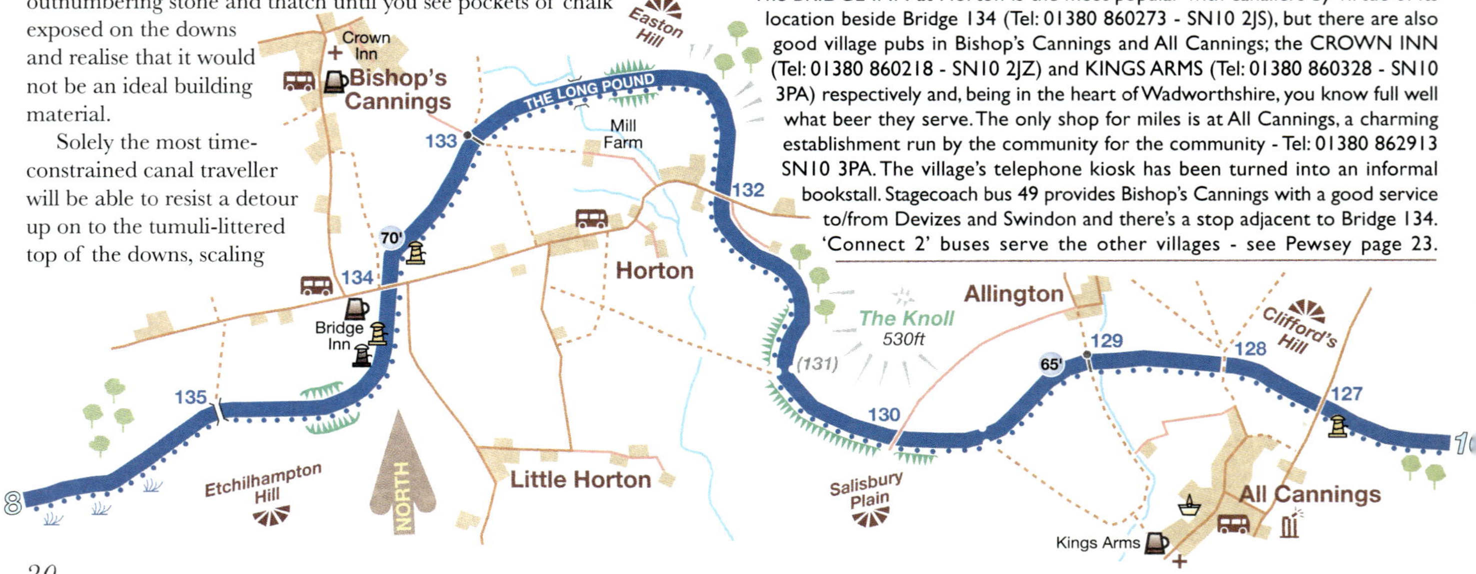

THE Long Pound continues its lazy traverse of the Vale of Pewsey, observed by the chiselled escarpments of the Marlborough Downs to the north and Salisbury Plain to the south. A characteristic of the Kennet & Avon seems to be the number of boat dwellers it attracts, escapees from authority in a bureaucratic black hole between Bath and Reading. Alton Barnes White Horse is readily visible from the canal to the north in the vicinity of Honeystreet. It was cut in 1812, though not without some delay after the original contractor decamped with the money. This part of Wiltshire is well known for its Crop Circles some of the most mysterious appearances of these strange configurations have occurred in the vicinity of Alton Barnes. You wouldn't be human (as opposed to alien), however, if you didn't wonder what came first ... the circles or the 'croppies'?

Overlooked by a high, red brick chimney, Honey Street Wharf was owned by Robbins, Lane & Pinniger, the last regular commercial users of the canal between Avonmouth and Hungerford. Their barge *Unity* carried softwood from Avonmouth and timber from Hungerford to the Honeystreet Wharf sawmill. The company also built many of the boats used on the K& A, Basingstoke Canal and River Wey prior to leaving the site in the late 1940s. The Barge Inn (not to be confused for a rendezvous with the one at Seend (Map 7) played an even more significant role in the life of Honeystreet Wharf, being an important stabling point for boat horses, a bakery, a brewery and a slaughterhouse all rolled into one. Following a destructive fire in 1858, it was completely rebuilt within six months, testimony to its importance to canal trade and commerce.

Near Bridge 123 there's a memorial to two airmen killed when their Albemarle bomber crashed in the vicinity in 1944. We had to brave the presence of a frisky bull to pay homage to them.

Chalky hills close in - Woodborough and Picked being less than half a mile from the canal - as you drift languidly past Wilcot, well known for its 'Wide Water' and its 'Ladies Bridge'. In an echo of events at Tixall Wide on the Trent & Mersey Canal, John Rennie collided with the intransigence of Lady Susannah Wroughton, who insisted that the canal cut through her grounds had to be in the guise of an ornamental lake. Ladies Bridge (120) at the western end of the Wide was an additional forelock-tug to the gentility. Bridge 116 is another gem, being a slender suspension footbridge privately erected for Colonel Wroughton in 1845 to the design of James Dredge, previously encountered on Map 4.

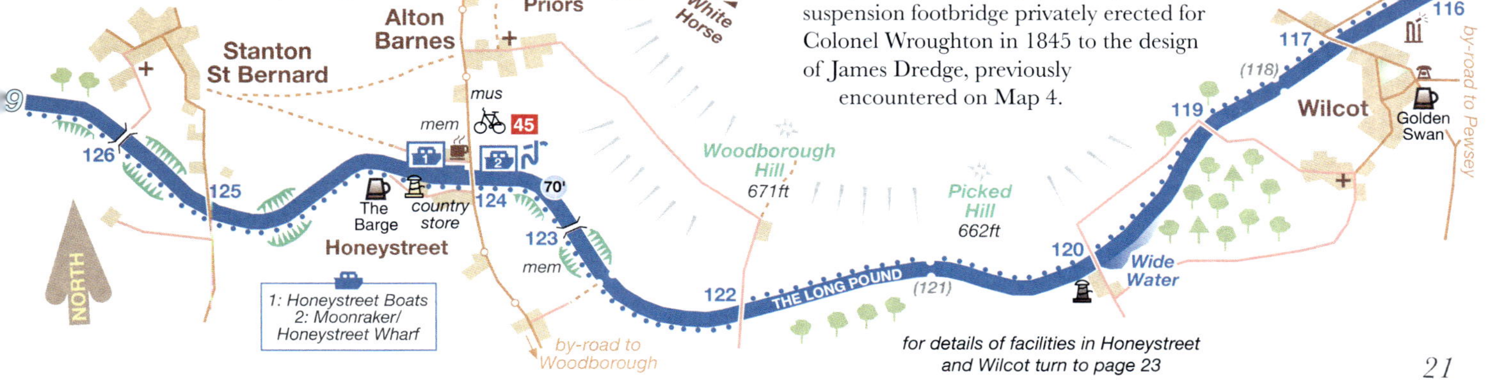

for details of facilities in Honeystreet and Wilcot turn to page 23

NEVER knowingly repetitive, the Kennet & Avon glides serenely from one landscape to the next in a sequence of scene changes so subtle that none outstays its welcome. No sooner have you fallen deeply in love with the Vale of Pewsey than you are being asked to bid it reluctantly farewell; or so it feels, especially when travelling eastwards.

Pewsey Wharf lies three-quarters of a mile from, and some fifty feet above, the place it purports to serve. Those statistics would have been of little import to George III's subjects and neither should they deter you from visiting what is a charming, if unassuming little town to this day. Why, it even has a River Avon running through it, though not the Avon in the title of this canal; Pewsey's Avon heads south through Salisbury to meet the sea at Christchurch. Pewsey Wharf boasts boating facilities and a pay & display car park.

Overlooked to the north by the provocatively bare, rounded shoulders of Martinsell Hill (947ft), and to the south by the enigmatic ramparts of Salisbury Plain, the canal considers its options, like a map-reading rambler, and elects to start climbing out of the Vale. In doing so, it is joined by the main line railway from the West Country to London, an almost constant companion for the remainder of your journey to Reading.

Boon companions they may become, but the Great Western Railway was demonstratively unkind to the Kennet & Avon. It bought it out in 1852 and allowed it to languish, though theoretically it remained open to navigation until Nationalisation in 1948, following which the British Transport Commission crassly advocated closing it. Were it not for the tub-thumping of enthusiasts thereafter the canal would have been criminally abandoned. In fact, the only time that authority appears to have valued it was during the Second World War when it became part of the eponymous Ironside* Line of defence in the event of invasion. You'll have spotted plenty of pillboxes already, but at Wootton Rivers there's a more substantial gun emplacement overlooking the canal, redolent of similar structures still to be found in northern France. Built to withstand heavy shelling and manned by the Home Guard, who did we think we were kidding, Mr Hitler?

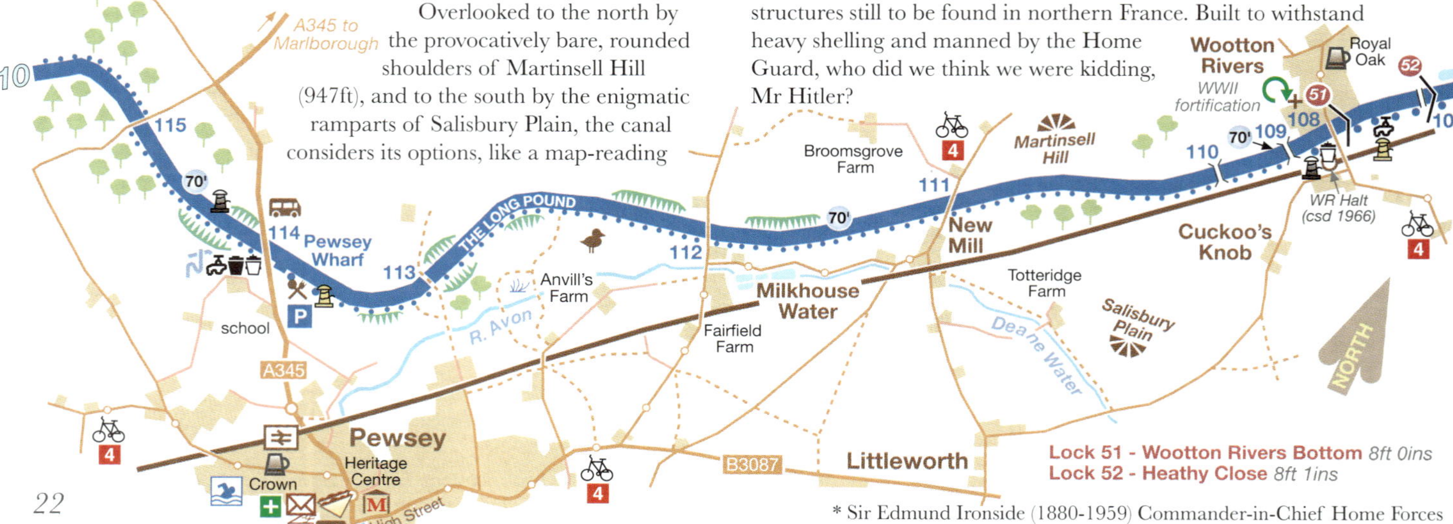

* Sir Edmund Ironside (1880-1959) Commander-in-Chief Home Forces

The Altons   Map 10

These peaceful neighbours beneath the Marlborough Downs are notable for their churches: Alton Barnes' St Mary's being of Saxon origin, whilst Alton Priors' slightly later period All Saints is in the tender care of the Churches Conservation Trust: the yew in its churchyard is said to be 1,700 years old! Wander up from Honeystreet and on the way you'll encounter Ray Pope's disarmingly trustworthy display of village photographs, social history at its most poignant and enchanting. Did we say peaceful? In 1830 gangs of disgruntled agricultural workers marched through the vale destroying new-fangled threshing machines in their path. Five score years and ten later, an aerodrome was built to train pilots in the arts of war. Of the latter only an air raid shelter remains, together with a memorial to five who didn't get to face the enemy.

Wilcot   Map 10

Lots of thatched properties in evidence, grouped about a sizeable green curiously sporting just one set of goalposts. The GOLDEN SWAN is a lovely thatched Wadworth pub - Tel: 01672 562289. Food, accommodation. SN9 5NN

Honeystreet   Map 10

THE BARGE INN - canalside. Tel: 01672 851222. Iconic status has not saved this famous Kennet & Avon pub from periods of uncertainty and temporary closure in recent years. To be on the safe side telephone ahead to check current status if you plan to rely on refreshment here. Music evenings/camping. SN9 5PS
HONEYSTREET MILL CAFE - Old Builder's Wharf. Tel: 01672 851853. Mother and son run canalside cafe open daily (Tuesdays excepted) from 9.30am-5pm. Crop Circle Exhibition and The India Shop. SN9 5PS

Pewsey   Map 11

Focus of its fecund vale, Pewsey admirably repays the trouble taken to walk down from the wharf. Personally, we feel that after a long stint at the tiller, the walk can only be good for you. Passing under the railway - whose well-kept station is a railhead for miles around - one comes at length to Marshall's Bakery, the first welcome outlier of civilisation. A weatherbeaten statue depicting King Alfred (but erected to show local approval of the crowning of King George V) marks the right-angled commencement of High Street which crosses a pretty stream with a sandy bed, no less than the 'Hampshire' Avon. Usually quite restful, Pewsey comes riotously to life for a fortnight in September when the Carnival takes place. The parish church has an ancient clock and some fine stained glass. A mile to the south, Pewsey's white horse was cut to commemorate the coronation of George VI. It is the smallest of Wiltshire's eight white horses.

Eating & Drinking

CROWN INN - Wilcot Road. Tel: 01672 562653. Cosy pub which brews its own World's End ales. Food restricted to Friday evening and Sun lunch. SN9 5EL
THE WATERFRONT - Pewsey Wharf. Tel: 01672 564020. Homely bar and bistro serving nourishing meals and local ales in old wharf building. SN9 5NU
SHED ALEHOUSE - North Street. Tel: 0776 981 2643. Congenial micropub serving a wide range of real ales, pilsners, ciders, wines and gins plus bar snacks. Closed Mon & Tue. SN9 5EX
TALE OF SPICE - North Street. Tel: 01672 564933. Indian restaurant and take-away. SN7 5ES
Chinese (offering fish & chips), kebab/pizza outlet and several cafes/tea rooms.

Shopping

Co-op supermarket, Spar convenience store, newsagent, bakery, post office and pharmacy. Small market on Tuesdays, and Farmers' Market on the 2nd Thursday monthly.

Things to Do

HERITAGE CENTRE - Avonside Works. Tel: 01672 562617. Entertaining collection of local history housed in Whatley & Hiscock's former agricultural engineering works. W&H were patentee's of pump and valve designs and the workshops, which date from circa 1870, were located in Pewsey to take advantage of the transport opportunities presented by the canal and the railway. Open Mon-Sat, 10am-4pm. Admission free, though small donations welcome. SN9 5AF
VALE COMMUNITY CAMPUS - Wilcot Road. Tel: 01380 826288. Swimming Pool. SN9 5EL

Connections

BUSES - Salisbury 'Red' X5 runs hourly to/from Swindon and Salisbury; and usually being operated by double-deckers, offers scenic views across the downland landscape. Tel: 0871 200 223. 'Connect 2' services 100/101 run to/from Devizes - to book seats telephone 01722 326154.
TRAINS - Great Western Railway services to/from Hungerford, Newbury, Reading and London Paddington with connections at Westbury for Trowbridge, Bradford and Bath. Tel: 0345 748 4950.

Wootton Rivers   Map 11

Idyllic canalside village boasting an excellent inn called the ROYAL OAK (Tel: 01672 810332 - SN8 4NQ) delightfully constructed of weatherboarding and thatch. Wadworth beers and guest ales, extensive menu and bed & breakfast. The quaint little church of St Andrew boasts an unusual clock, made by the local blacksmith in 1911 to commemorate the coronation of George V. One of its three faces spells out GLORY BE TO GOD in place of numerals.

SOMEONE ought to write a book about canal summits: their generic traits, their inherent variety. Not only did the 18th century engineers have to climb, when they got to the top they had to find water. The Kennet & Avon's two mile summit does not present too many opportunities for water storage and is obviously hardly long enough to act as a linear reservoir. The solution came from Wilton Water, a small reservoir fed by springs, and a pair of pumping engines were provided to feed the summit. Two centuries later, little has changed other than provision of new electric pumps and preservation of the old steam monsters who originally did the work, more of which in a moment.

Meanwhile consider the summit itself. Burbage Wharf was built in the nineteenth century to handle trade from Marlborough, which never received its promised branch canal. The wharf's crane was fully restored in 2010 and sits handsomely canalside dreaming of cargoes which might one day return. In its heyday it handled copious quantities of timber, stone, coal and agricultural produce.

Burbage Bridge (No.104), carrying the busy A338 Marlborough-Andover road, is an early example of a skew bridge, ie one that crosses the canal at an angle rather than at ninety degrees. John Rennie is thought to have been the first canal engineer to master the skew technique and further K&A examples include Beech Grove Bridge (No 98) at Crofton and Mill Bridge (No 97) at Great Bedwyn. The railway also had a goods facility at Burbage which had originally been conceived as an interchange point between the two transport modes. Once, however, the railway had provided a branch line to Marlborough, use of the siding settled down to spasmodic cattle trains run in connection with cattle fairs.

There were *two* railway lines linking Savernake (pronounced Sava-*nack*) with Marlborough, a Great Western branch which terminated in the town and the Midland & South Western Railway, which was part of a through route between Southampton and Cheltenham. The former's Low Level station has vanished, though the line, of course, remains busy. The High Level station on the latter line is more or less intact and used domestically, its occupants having imaginatively created a linear water feature between the platforms, whilst the old signal box and a water tower can be glimpsed from the path across the canal tunnel. Incidentally, the famous Gresley record-holder, *Mallard*, had to be

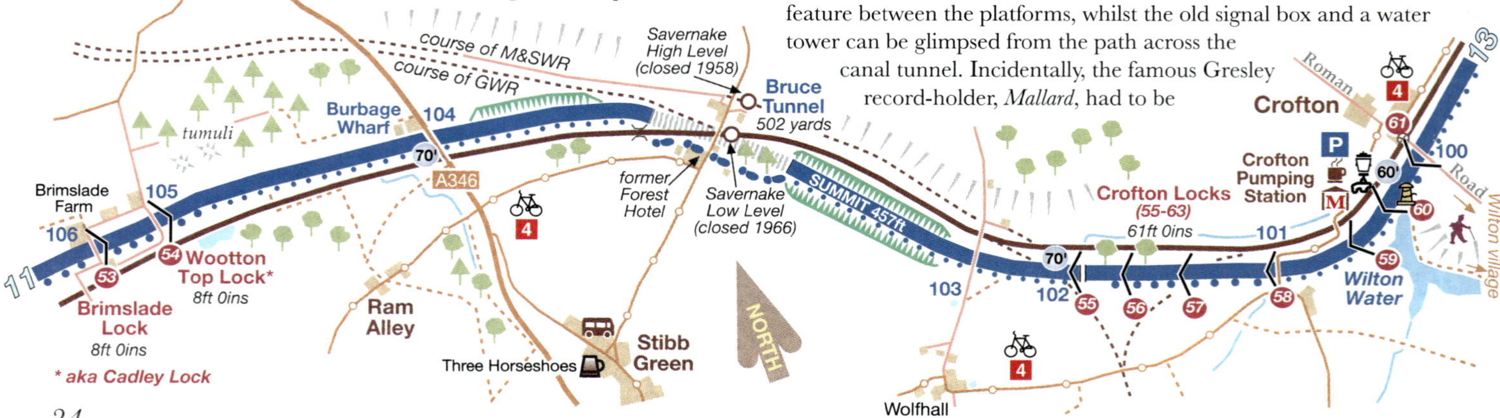

ignominiously shunted into a siding at Savernake Low Level in 1948 after developing a defect whilst taking part in the Locomotive Exchanges which marked the beginning of the nationalised railway era.

Savernake, which occupies much of the landscape between the canal and the town of Marlborough to the north, extends to 4,500 acres and is the only privately owned forest in Britain, belonging to the Earl of Cardigan. A Grand Avenue of beech trees was planted by Capability Brown. Less than a mile north of the canal stands the Ailesbury Column erected to give thanks for the recovery of George III from madness. The canal dives headlong into Bruce Tunnel, named after Thomas Bruce, the Earl of Ailesbury, who owned much of the land in the vicinity. It was perhaps ironic that the Kennet & Avon Canal Company should name the tunnel thus, for it was only on the good Earl's insistence that it had to be built at all. A deep cutting would doubtless have coped with the low hill standing in the canal's way. At 502 yards long and wide enough for two narrowboats to pass inside, it's the only one worthy of the name on the entire K&A, and has no towpath, working boatmen pulling their craft through by chains fixed to the wall whilst their horses crossed above. Pedestrians still use the old horse path, of course, and, as is so often the case, are treated to much that the boater misses. The former Savernake Forest Hotel for example, built to serve the railway, but closed at the end of the 20th century and converted into housing, though reputedly still haunted by a black dog.

The tunnel's eastern portal is slightly more imposing than its western counterpart and carries a memorial plaque to Thomas Bruce. As its approach cutting fades away Bridge 103 carries a lane southwards to Wolfhall where Jane Seymour, Henry VIII's third wife was born in 1508. Hilary Mantel used the name as the title of her Booker Prize-winning novel.

All too quickly, the summit level is done with. Observe the feeder channel from Wilton Water and the remains of the bridges carrying the lines of the Midland & South Western Junction Railway across the canal as you approach the Crofton flight. Here nine locks drop you down by some sixty feet amidst the gently rolling hills that have become the canal's trademark.

Crofton Pumping Station is famous enough to require little introduction, being one of the Kennet & Avon's 'must see' highlights. Initial proposals were for a lower and longer (eighteen-mile) summit level with a 4,300 yard tunnel extending almost to Wootton Rivers, but these were amended on the advice of William Jessop, which was readily accepted by John Rennie; hence the need for pumps to raise water from Wilton Water up forty feet to the higher summit. Two steam engines manfully did the job until 1959 when the removal of the top twenty feet of the pumphouse chimney resulted in insufficient draught for the boilers and they were replaced by first a diesel pump and then an electric one. The Crofton Society painstakingly restored the steam pumps and the building*, which was officially reopened by Sir John Betjeman in August 1970.

*Plus, subsequently, the chimney to its full height at the behest of Sir John Smith.

Crofton   Map 12

Crofton Pumping Station houses two Cornish beam engines, the oldest built by Boulton & Watt dating from 1812, its junior a Harvey's of Hayle engine of 1845. Steam is raised through a hand-stoked, coal fired Lancashire boiler. Between them, the two engines can lift two tons of water to the summit at every stroke. Wilton Water was enlarged into a reservoir in 1836 and has become rich in birdlife. The pumping station is open to the public daily from Easter to the end of September, whilst the machinery itself comes to life on selected weekends - Tel: 01672 870300 for further information. There is a cafe and souvenir shop too. SN8 3DW

A Roman Road makes up part of a charming circular walk based on Crofton. The *Venta Belgarum* once linked Winchester with Marlborough, now it will take you from the canal to Wilton Windmill returning, for the sake of variety, along the footpath bordering Wilton Water

Wilton   (Map 12)

Thatched cottages by a duckpond and a chapel.

Eating & Drinking

THE SWAN - Tel: 01672 870274. Lovely country inn. SN8 3SS

Things to Do

WILTON WINDMILL - Tel: 01672 870594. Dates from 1821 and is now alliteratively promoted as 'the only working windmill in Wessex'. Open Sun & BH Mon, Easter to September, 2-5pm. SN8 3SW

13 KENNET & AVON CANAL The Bedwyns 4mls/8lks/3hrs

THIS is a quintessential length of the Kennet & Avon, much frequented by photographers and artists anxious to capture images of the canal in its propinquity to the Great Western main line. You might argue that the railway's cast list lacks variety nowadays - it would have been nice to have been here when the *Cornish Riviera Express* was still entrusted to 'Kings' (or even 'Westerns', 'Warships' or 'Fifties') - but there is still a thrill to be experienced as the canal traveller is overtaken by the present generation of dark green IET bi-modes or, better still, by one of the lengthy stone trains which appear intent on moving the Mendips piecemeal to Greater London.

The Battle of Bedwyn was fought here in 675 between Escuin, a West Saxon nobleman who had seized the throne of Queen Saxburga, and the redoubtable King Wulfhere of Mercia. The fighting was fierce and the loss of life substantial before Escuin forced King Wulfhere to retreat northwards. The battle to restore this section of the Kennet & Avon Canal was far less bloody and ended with all the locks between Crofton and Hungerford being reopened by 1988.

Great Bedwyn Wharf is unusual in that it was built on the towpath side. Whilst never handling as much trade as Burbage Wharf, three miles to the west, it once accommodated two coal merchants and was still shipping wheat to Aldermaston

until just before the First World War. The Bruce Trust offer canal boating opportunities to the disabled.

The origins of Bedwyn Dyke are shrouded in the mists of time, but one plausible explanation is that it is part of the much greater Wansdyke, a 5th century fortification erected in two distinct parts across the West Country The remnants here lie within a stone's throw of Burnt Mill Lock which was originally called Knight's Mill Lock, gaining its new name after Great Bedwyn water mill was destroyed by fire early in the 19th century. Two hundred years on, one mischievously wonders if it was 'an insurance job' following the reduction in flow associated with the advent of the canal. However, the infant River Dun certainly adds to the scene as the canal proceeds past Little Bedwyn which is where all the photographers like to gather. If they are out in numbers, their presence may well indicate the imminent appearance of a steam-hauled special.

The lazy, lockless miles of the Long Pound are but a distant memory now as the locks come along thick and fast. But there's a delightful timelessness about this little known corner of East Wiltshire that puts you in no mood to hurry.

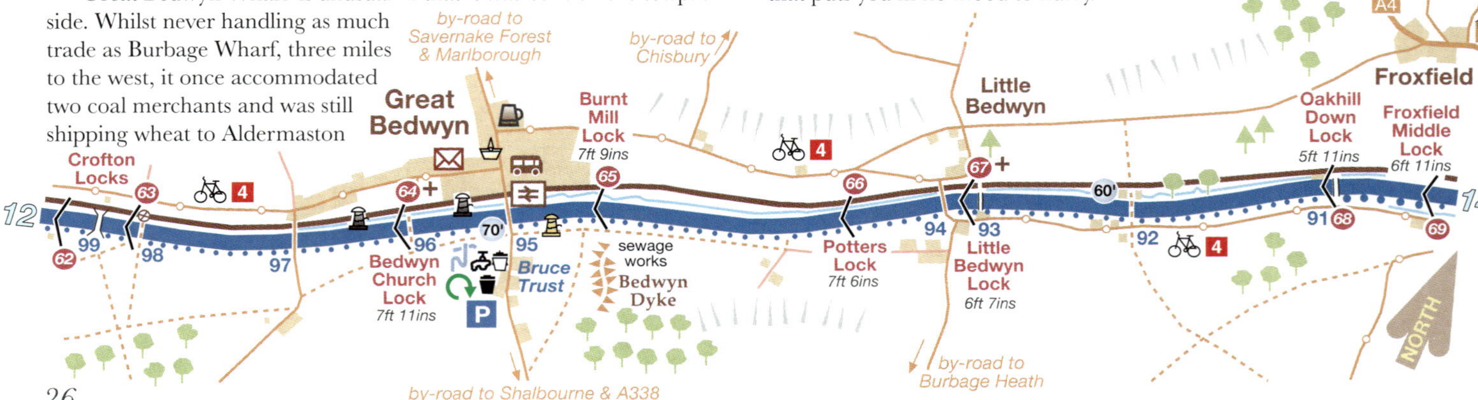

Great Bedwyn
Map 13

One senses Great Bedwyn was a more important place in the past, at one time it returned two Members of Parliament! Nowadays it lies at the western edge of London's commuter belt - First Great Western's outer suburban service terminates here when, if they hadn't ripped up the track even before Beeching, Marlborough might have made more sense. In the substantial church lies the tomb of Sir John Seymour, Jane's father - see page 25.

Eating & Drinking
THREE TUNS - High Street. Tel: 01672 870280. Award-winning gastropub open daily for lunch and dinner ex Mons. SN8 3NU

Shopping
Village stores open daily 6.30am (7.30 Sat & Sun) - 8pm (2pm Sun) and picturesque Post Office with examples of now deceased local stonemason's art. We trust he carved a good one for himself.

Connections
BUSES - service 20 operates Mon-Sat to/from Marlborough and Hungerford. Tel: 0871 200 2233. TRAINS - Great Western Railway provide useful services running to/from Paddington via Hungerford/Kintbury/Newbury providing incremental succour for towpath walkers. Tel: 0345 748 4950.

Little Bedwyn
Map 13

St Michael's Church is built of local flint and completes a charming scene. Sir Felix Pole, celebrated General Manager of the Great Western Railway in the nineteen-twenties, was born in Little Bedwyn in 1877 and buried here in 1956.

Froxfield
Maps 13/14

THE PELICAN - Bath Road, Froxfield (access via Bridge 90). Tel: 01488 682479. 17th century coaching inn on the old Bath Road offering comfortable accommodation, lunch and dinner Mon-Fri and food from noon Sat & Sun. SN8 3JY

Hungerford
Map 14

Virtually equidistant from Oxford and Salisbury, Hungerford's broad, sloping High Street strides confidently down to the canal, concealing the fact that the town is comparatively small. Nevertheless, it comes alive at least once a year on the occasion of the 'Hocktide Ceremony' (held on the second Tuesday following Easter) whereupon ninety-nine commoners are summoned to the Town Hall by the blowing of a horn. Two 'Tuttimen' are elected and proceed from house to house exchanging oranges for kisses.

Eating & Drinking
ELIANE - High Street. Tel: 01488 686100. Stylishly appointed coffee shop; scrumptious cakes! Open from 8.30am weekdays, 9am Sat and 10am Sun. RG17 0NF
JOHN O' GAUNT - Bridge Street (to north of canal). Tel: 01488 683535. *Good Beer Guide* listed inn offering a good choice of food and real ales, plus a connoisseur's choice of bottled Belgian beer. RG17 0EG
TUTTI POLE - High Street (adjacent Bridge 84). Tel: 01488 682515. Coffees, lunches and teas served by a bevy of attentive and comely waitresses. RG17 0DN

Shopping
Hungerford has become a centre for the antiques trade, the Arcade and Below Stairs (up past the railway bridge) being prime examples of this new focus of commerce. Hungerford Bookshop (just past the Italianate Town Hall) is excellent for both new and secondhand titles, and there's a wine merchant called The Naked Grape. Wednesday is market day, and there's a monthly food & artisan market on selected Sundays. The Post Officce is in W. H. Smith on High Street. On the A4 west of the town, and accessible on foot from Bridge 88, Cobbs Farm Shop (inc: butcher, fishmonger & cafe) is highly recommended. Tel: 01488 686770. RG17 0SP

Connections
BUSES - service 20 operates infrequently Mon-Sat to/from Marlborough via the railhead at Bedwyn. Service 90 operates Mon-Sat to/from the racehorsey town of Lambourn and Swindon. Tel: 0871 200 2233. TRAINS - useful Great Western Railway services along the Kennet corridor. Tel: 0345 748 4950. TAXIS - Hungerford Taxis. Tel: 01488 580002.

Kintbury
Map 15

A delightful village with a notable church within which a tablet commemorates Charles Dundas, recording that he represented the County of Berks in 'ten successive Parliaments in full possession of every faculty'. Not many politicians, we would tentatively suggest, can claim that for even one. There is also a memorial to Sir Gordon Richards who won the 1953 Epsom Derby on Pinza.

Eating & Drinking
DUNDAS ARMS - canalside Bridge 75. Tel: 01488 658263. Much loved waterside inn named after the first Chairman of the Kennet & Avon Canal Company. Good food and accommodation. RG17 9UT
BLUE BALL - village centre. Tel: 01488 608126. Cosy pub offering wood fired pizzas. RG17 9T
RED HOUSE - Marsh Benham. Tel: 01635 582017. Charming pub/restaurant of brick and thatch. Open daily from noon and a nice stroll across the railway from Bridge 68 (Map 16). RG20 8LY.

Shopping
Convenience store (with PO counter) and bakery.

Connections
BUSES - service 3 to/from Hungerford and Newbury. TRAINS - as Hungerford. Tel: 0345 748 4950.

WILTSHIRE morphs into Berkshire. At the snail's pace inherent in canal travel the significance of the old county boundaries is as it should be, a fundamental matter of tradition and identity. Bridge 90 offers access to Froxfield village which boasts a remarkable group of almshouses known as the Duchess of Somerset's Hospital.

A change of county brings a change of mood as the A4 trunk road comes alongside the waterway to shake it out of its sleepy complacency. Fortunately, however, much of the old Bath Road's traffic has been siphoned off by the M4 motorway and it's not as fearfully busy as it once was. In any case, the K&A maintains its dignity as it makes its unruffled way eastwards accompanied by the River Dun which it crosses on a compact three-arched aqueduct above Cobbler's Lock.

Hungerford Marsh Lock is equipped with a swing bridge across the lock chamber, reminding well-travelled canallers of a similar juxtaposition at Fenny Stratford on the Grand Union. The bridge was provided for the benefit of the commoners who enjoyed - and for that matter still do - rights over Freeman's Marsh, across which the canal

journeys in company with the River Dun and the railway.

Hungerford's imposing parish church of St Lawrence overlooks swing-bridge 85. Are there any churches closer to a canal? Kidderminster perhaps, but we forgot to bring a tape measure. For well over a hundred years Hungerford Wharf was occupied by J. Wooldridge & Son, builders, who were also responsible, from 1851-63, for the maintenance of the K&A between Wootton Rivers and Reading. They finally left the site in 1962. Tom and Angela Rolt sojourned here aboard *Cressy* at the outbreak of the Second World War.

In tandem with the crystal clear waters of the River Dun, the K&A crosses Hungerford Common, where commoners rights were granted by John O' Gaunt, father of King Henry IV, back in the fourteenth century. At Dun Mill Lock, confluence of the Dun and the Kennet, a couple of former mills have been converted into highly desirable residences. See how clear the Kennet is here. Further downstream, as it becomes navigable, turbidity becomes a problem, in other words you can't see the bottom from the top; much like life itself.

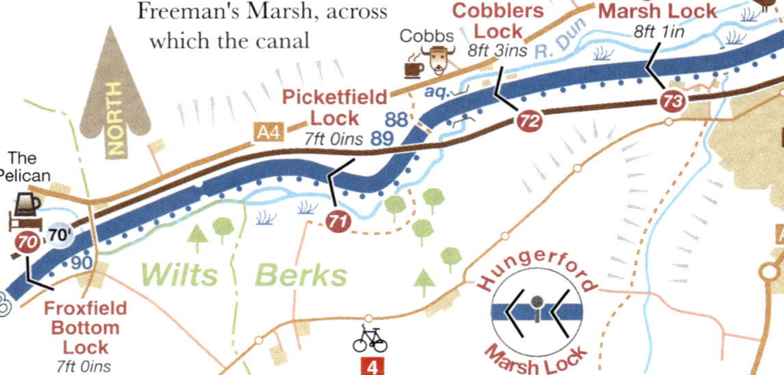

for details of facilities at Hungerford turn back to page 27

AT Kintbury the Kennet sidles up to the canal and makes it an offer it can't refuse. Thenceforth, at increasing intervals, the river and the canal merge and boaters need to have their wits about them, as cross-currents occur, especially after significant rainfall.

Received wisdom that the best scenery belongs to the K&A west of Hungerford, and that it continues to get better the further you go in the direction of Bath, is belied by the beauty of the Kennet's watermeadows. This is a mouth-watering length of navigation, as tasty as the watercress once grown in the extensive beds bordering the waterway between Hungerford and Kintbury, and punted downstream for onward transportation by rail. The cress farm has long since disappeared, overwhelmed by competition from larger growers in Hampshire and Dorset.

It was at Kintbury in June 1797 that the first section of the K&A was officially opened by its then chairman Charles Dundas, who was present to greet a military band transported along the cut from Newbury to lend an air of jollity to the proceedings. For a century or so Kintbury Wharf thrived, handling large quantities of iron and coke destined for several local ironworks, as well as raw materials for the nearby brewery. Following the canal's commercial decline and subsequent restoration, Kintbury took centre stage again in December 1972 when Miss W. Rennie, a descendant of John Rennie, officially reopened Kintbury Lock. This stretch of canal appeared in the novelist Robert Goddard's thriller *Sight Unseen*.

Unruffled by the outside world, the canal glides cheerily along in a world of its own, past the slopes of Irish Hill. This was once the site of a curious industry, chalk from the hill being gathered for the manufacture of whiting, a powder used in the production of paint. There were at one time five whiting mills in the Kintbury area, which sent their finished products along the canal to Bristol until the 1930s. Follow the footpath from Bridge 73 to the crest of Irish Hill for fine views southwards over the Hampshire Downs.

Copse Lock is captivatingly located at the foot of a conifer wood. At its tail the Kennet comes swaggering in. Those familiar with the music of Gerald Finzi might find it entering their heads. Finzi lived at Ashmansworth to the south of Newbury and founded the Newbury String Players during the Second World War. Inspired by articles in *The Observer* by William Bliss, Finzi canoed the K&A in 1930.

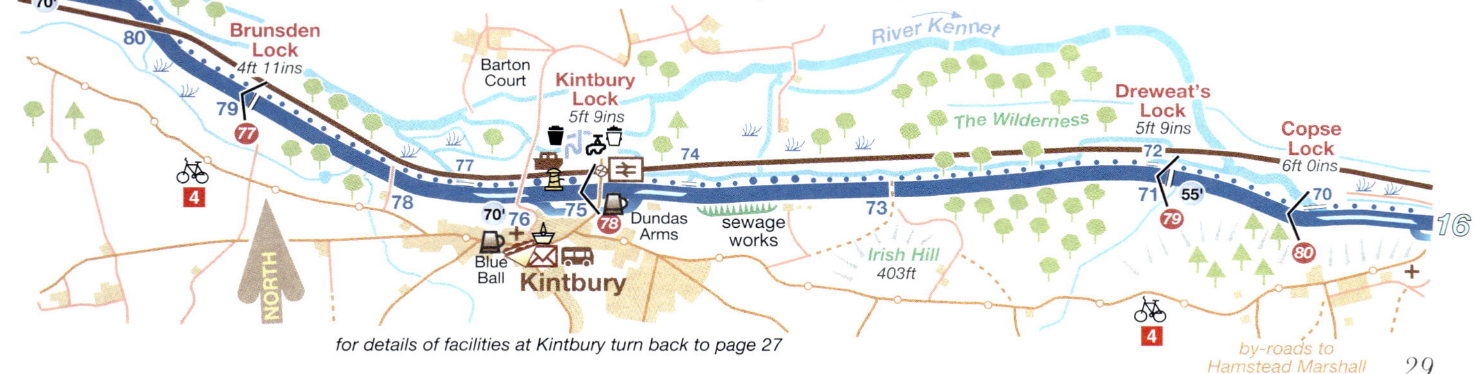

for details of facilities at Kintbury turn back to page 27

THE Kennet has Site of Special Scientific Interest status and in such circumstances the boater feels privileged to be granted access and should respond with according deference. Skirting a former Norman deer park - which contains the remains of no less than three motte & bailey castles - the canal widens cosmetically to form Benham Broad. Glimpsed through woodland to the north, Benham Park is an 18th century mansion (now used as offices) designed by Henry Holland with grounds (where polo is now played) by Capability Brown.

The battle of Newbury's Bypass in 1996 seems as ancient history now as the battles which took place hereabouts during the Civil War. How long before the Sealed Knot offer re-enactments? But a generation has been nurtured oblivious to the heroics of 'Swampy' and his fellow tree-dwellers and the A34's crossing of the Kennet & Avon Canal below Higg's Lock seems almost innocuous; why, the bridge has even won an award - from those peerless arbiters of taste, The Concrete Society! One day, you can bet your bottom dollar, the by-pass will lie as derelict as the trackbeds of the old railway lines to Lambourn and to Southampton; all that remains of the former's bridging of the canal is a red-brick abutment on the offside.

Most canals find their way surreptitiously around the unappealing posteriors of the places they encounter, but at Newbury the town is sliced quite literally and picturesquely in half by the waterway which threads so delightfully through it; though whilst there is much to see, the boater has to keep their wits about them. West Mills Wharf (Bridge 62) was once a hive of activity, handling, amongst other commodities, coal from the Somerset collieries. Its last commercial use came in 1950 when a cargo of salt from Middlewich was delivered by John Knill.

Newbury Lock (cheek by jowl with the imposing parish church of St Nicholas) was the first to be completed, in 1796, on the Newbury-Bath section of the canal. Uniquely on the K&A, it is equipped with lever-operated ground paddles of a type relatively common on northern canals, where they are referred to as cloughs. Regrettably, for the connoisseur of the obscure, they appear to be padlocked out of regular use. Beside the lock a small plaque, unveiled in 1997, pays tribute to the late John Gould MBE, founder member of the Kennet & Avon Canal Trust and former working boatman, who died in March 1999. "Without him there would be no K&A Canal."

Ambushed by the skittish waters of the Kennet and a mill stream, the navigation

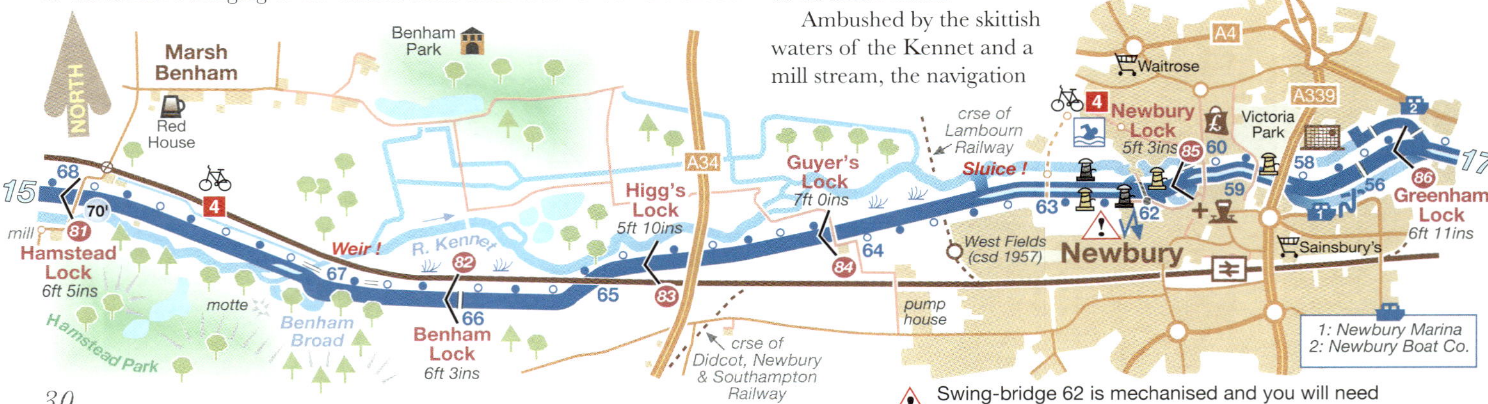

Swing-bridge 62 is mechanised and you will need both a 'Watermate' key and windlass to operate it.

proceeds under Town Bridge - a stylish, single-arched stone structure dating from 1770. Being the terminus of the original Kennet Navigation, it was built without a towpath, which presented problems for horse-drawn craft, especially as it was forbidden for horses to haul across the main road. The solution involved a special float, kept by the lock; whilst the barge was tied below the bridge and the horse by the lock, the float was attached to the tow rope and allowed to drift down below the bridge to the barge. Then once the horse started pulling the barge would move through the bridge and into the lock: the natural flow downstream normally being sufficient to carry the vessel through the bridge. Moorings are provided at Victoria Park (although we consider West Mills to be a nicer place to spend the night), directly opposite Newbury Wharf. Originally the terminal wharf of the Kennet Navigation, this was one of the busiest wharves on the K&A, but most of it disappeared under, in chronological order, a bus station, car park and the main Inner Relief road. Sometimes you come to the inescapable conclusion that you are two centuries too late to see the canals at their best. The two-storeyed Stone Wharf Building survives, however, and serves as a tea room.

Newbury

Map 16

Few towns embrace the inland waterways on their doorstep as affectionately and publically as Newbury. Northbrook Street, the main shopping thoroughfare, is carried across the navigation enabling a quick shop to be done while your boat is worked through Newbury Lock. Look out for the imposing church of St Nicholas built in the 16th century by a wealthy Newbury wool merchant. On 25th June 1811, in a demonstration of 'manufacturing celerity' the celebrated 'Newbury Coat' was tailored from wool shorn in the morning from two sheep and worn by Sir John Throckmorton 13 hours and 20 minutes later.

Eating & Drinking

COTE - Northbrook Street. Tel: 01635 35315. Reliable French brasserie handily placed near Bridge 60 and open from 8am (9am Sun). RG14 1AA

COW & CASK - Inches Yard, Market Street. Tel: 0751 765 8071. *Good Beer Guide* listed micropub, local ales, pickled eggs and pork pies. RG14 5DP

LOCK STOCK & BARREL - Northbrook Street (Bridge 60). Tel: 01635 580550. Fullers (of Chiswick) pub with waterside terrace. RG14 1AA

MIO FIORE - Inches Yard, Market Street. Tel: 01635 552023. Friendly and authentic Italian. RG14 5DP

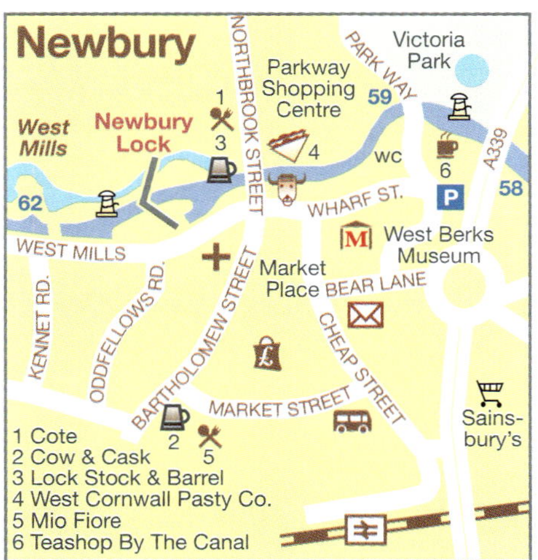

TEASHOP BY THE CANAL - The Wharf. Tel: 01635 522609. Breakfasts, lunches and teas. RG14 5AS
Nip into the West Cornwall Pasty Co while the lock fills! Lots of chain restaurants such as Nando's, Ask and Cafe Rouge supplement independently owned establishments.

Shopping

A most amenable town to shop in with all facilities very close to the canal. Don't miss the opportunity to purchase some Newbury Sausage from Griffins butchers overlooking Town Bridge (No.60). On Batholomew Street, to the south of Bridge 60, stands Inn at Home, a marvellous beer shop which also deals in cider and wine. Markets on Thursdays and Saturdays. Farmers Markets on 1st and 3rd Sundays in the month; Artisans Market on the last Sunday of the month. Camp Hopson's department store on Northbrook Street owes its 1920s origins to the merger by marriage of two local retailing dynasties.

Things to Do

WEST BERKSHIRE MUSEUM - The Wharf. Tel: 01635 279279. Excellent local museum housed in former cloth hall and granary. Wed-Sun 10-4. RG14 5AS

Connections

TRAINS - Great Western Railway offer excellent services along the Kennet Valley with lots of stations creating handy towpath walks. Tel: 0345 748 4950.

BUSES - services supplement the trains along the Kennet Valley but also operate tantalisingly up on the Wiltshire and Berkshire downs. Tel: 0871 200 2233.

TAXIS - Newbury Taxis. Tel: 01635 44444.

17 KENNET & AVON CANAL Thatcham 4mls/5lks/3hrs

WELCOME to 'waterland'! That most mercurial of elements is all-pervading as the Kennet & Avon - half navvy-dug cut, half canalised river - makes its way across a marshy landscape intersected by slender drainage channels and brackish pools and backwaters. Breezes sigh through the bullrushes with the provocative rustle that petticoats used to make; a lost allurement mourned by red-blooded males of a certain age.

Business parks (Newbury is Vodafone's global headquarters) and the railway ensure that the canal traveller has no cognisance of the town's famous race course. Could the old heavy-treading boat-horses sense the presence of thoroughbreds nearby, and were they envious of these equine cousins' gilded lifestyles?

Out of sight to the south, Greenham's synonymy with nuclear missiles is fast eroding. The mass protests and the Women's Peace Camp, located less than a mile from the K&A, appear to belong to another, and perhaps more compassionate era.

The River Lambourn, a delightful trout stream which has flowed some fifteen miles from its source at the foot of the eponymous downs so well-known for the training of race horses, has its confluence with the Kennet in the vicinity of Ham Lock.

Thatcham Reedbeds are home to such rarities as Cetti's Warblers, Scarlet Tiger Moths and Desmoulin's Whorl Snails. Mesolithic tools have been unearthed in the rich peat substrata. A Discovery Centre, located close to Widmead Lock, offers the chance to explore this fascinating terrain along a number of designated paths.

At just over a mile, the Long Cut is the longest straight on the entire K&A. The cut leads on to Monkey Marsh Lock, one of the last remaining pair of examples of the turf-sided locks once prevalent on the Kennet Navigation. These had timber walled chambers to some two feet above the lock's lower level, above which their turf sides sloped away at an angle of 45 degrees. Whilst the locks were filling there was considerable water loss through the turf banks but copious supplies of water from the Kennet meant that this was not considered too problematic.

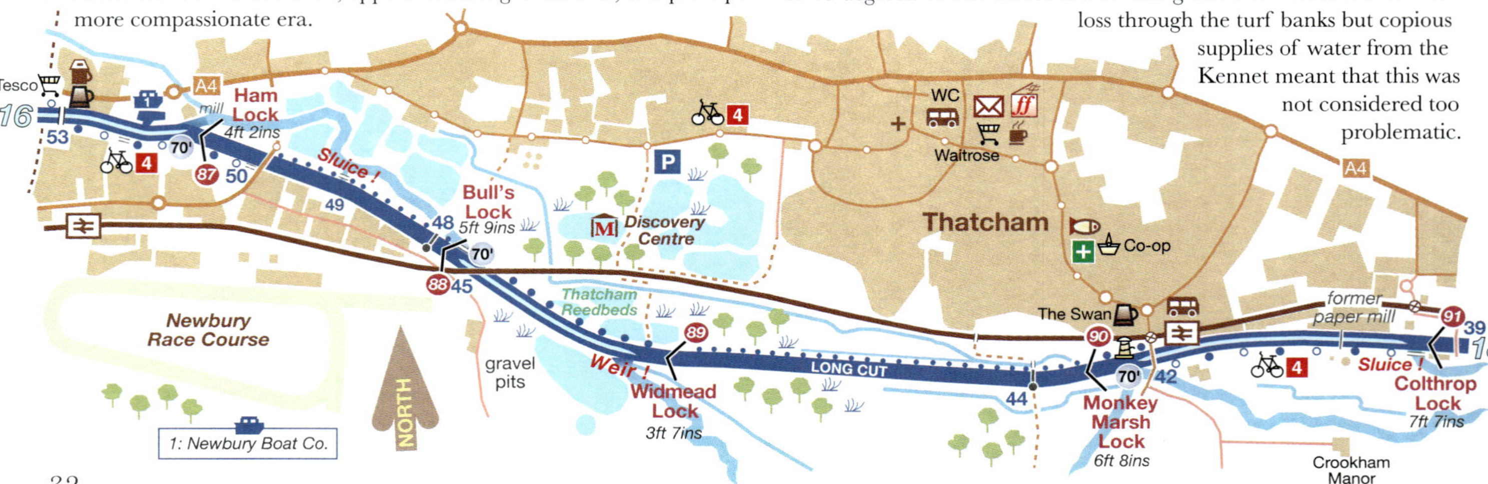

Thatcham
Map 17

If you feel like stretching your legs, Thatcham evinces a curious post Sixties charm about its town square. Almost the only building left of any antiquity is the church, though even that was 'violently restored' in 1852 according to Betjeman & Piper's *Architectural Guide to Berkshire*. A Millennium monument in the square salutes some of Thatcham's significant events, such as the arrival of electric light in 1920, the first telephone in 1912, and the Kennet Navigation in 1723, whilst, in 1160, Thatcham Market was attacked by a band of brigands from Newbury. Stirring stuff!

Eating & Drinking
SWAN HOTEL - Station Road. Tel: 01635 862084. Marston's 'all-day' pub offering accommodation also. Food from noon daily. RG19 4QL
Fish & chips within easy reach of the canal. Further pubs in the town centre, along with a Costa coffee shop and several ethnic restaurants and takeaways.

Shopping
There's a small Co-op within 5 minutes of the canal as well as a pharmacist. Most of the high street banks have branches in the town centre where you'll also find a Waitrose supermarket.

Connections
BUSES - 'Jet Black' service No.1 runs half-hourly (hourly Sun) to/from Newbury and Reading from Thatcham town centre stops. Connect services 104/5 offer an approx bi-hourly, Mon-Sat connection between the railway station and the town centre. Tel: 0871 200 2233.
TRAINS - Great Western Railway services to/from Newbury and Reading with useful stops at Midgham and Theale for towpath users. Tel: 0345 748 4950.
TAXIS - Kennet & Avon Cars. Tel: 01635 847853.

Woolhampton
Map 18

Former coaching village on the old Bath Road, suffering demolition when the road was widened. Douai Abbey can be accessed to the North. The Great Western Railway renamed the little station on Woolhampton's doorstep 'Midgham', concerned lest Woolhampton (as perhaps called out by porters in broad Berkshire dialect) be confused with Wolverhampton, the Black Country industrial centre.

Eating & Drinking
ROWBARGE - canalside, Bridge 31. Tel: 0118 971 2213. Fabulous Brunning & Price pub (they also own the excellent Corn Mill in Llangollen and The Wharf at Castlefield, Manchester). Open 11.30am. RG7 5SH
THE ANGEL - Bath Road. Tel: 0118 971 3827. Comfortable village centre inn. Breakfasts from 10am, lunch from noon, dinner from 5pm. RG7 5PT

Shopping
Charming village shop/cafe offering groceries and take-away food. Open from 7am (8am Sun).

Connections
TRAINS - Great Western trains. Remember that the station is called 'Midgham'! Tel: 0345 748 4950.
BUSES - 'Jet Black' service No.1 runs half-hourly (hourly Sun) to/from Newbury/Reading. Tel: 0871 200 2233.

Sulhamstead
Map 19

Dispersed village of five distinct entities. Grade 1 listed Folly Farm was designed by Edwin Lutyens in 1906. Gertrude Jekyll helped with the garden, and it is occasionally open to the public under the NGS.

Eating & Drinking
SPRING INN - Bath Road (accessible on foot from Bridge 23). Tel: 0118 930 3440. Comfortable pub. Regional beers and a wide range of food. RG7 5HP

Aldermaston Wharf
Map 19

A short waymarked trail will introduce you to Aldermaston Wharf's salient features including: the former transhipment arm, the lock, the lift-bridge, and the remains of an old brewery.

Eating & Drinking
BUTT INN - Station Road (a few hundred yards south of the canal at Aldermaston Bridge). Tel: 0118 971 3309. Open from 11.30am daily (noon Sun) RG7 4LA
TEA ROOMS - Wharfside. Tel: 0777 983 7065. Refreshments served in former canal employee's cottage. Open Thur-Sun. RG7 4JS

Connections
TRAINS - Great Western Railway electric services linking Newbury with Reading. Tel: 0345 748 4950.
BUSES - as Woolhampton

Theale
Map 19

Once a staging point for coaches on the Bath Road, Theale is quainter than Thatcham, and not such a long walk from the canal. Furthermore, Theale has a friendly air about it and an adequate choice of shops. Its church is an imposing example of Gothic Revival said to have been inspired by Salisbury Cathedral.

Eating & Drinking
At least two pubs, plus Chinese and Indian restaurants, and takeaways in the village centre.

Shopping
Co-op (6am-11pm), pharmacy, newsagent, post office, and bakery all located on the High Street seven or eight minutes stroll from the canal.

Connections
TRAINS - Great Western Railway trains link stations along the canal from Reading to Newbury. Tel: 0345 748 4950.

18 KENNET & AVON CANAL Woolhampton 4mls/3lks/3hrs

LOW-LYING, yet well-wooded, the navigation exudes great charm as it continues its undemonstrative way through the Kennet Valley. To the north, Bucklebury Common rises to over four hundred feet; to the south Crookham Common is almost as high: both form rewarding - not to say tempting - horizons.

Canals promoted, but never built, are almost of as much fascination to inland waterway historians as canals built but abandoned. The pound between Midgham and Heale's locks was earmarked as the egress for a link between the Kennet & Avon and Basingstoke canals in the 1820s, promoted as the Berks & Hants Junction Canal. Landowners and the Thames Commissioners (who would have lost trade had the canal been constructed) successfully defeated the scheme ... more's the pity.

To the north, prominent on the skyline, stands Midgham's lonely Victorian church. Swing-bridges abound: No.31, at Woolhampton, deserves care and attention when approached from upstream as, below the tail of the lock, the river makes a brisk entrance, and you must have your wits about you if you are not to be the cause of merriment (at best or *schadenfreude* at worst) amongst the patrons of the adjoining beer garden. Electrified now, the bridge poses no inherent problems in operation, but reflect that, in 1940, Tom and

Angela Rolt took three hours to negotiate their way past the bridge with the help of 'half the able-bodied men of the village heaving on crowbars under the direction of the red-faced landlord of the Rowbarge. On the same journey, the locks were in equally recalcitrant condition, and the Rolts were grateful for an abundance of reeds, bunches of which they heaved into the lock chambers to staunch the flow of water from heavily leaking gates. An earlier traveller and writer to explore the K&A had been Fred S. Thacker, whose book *Kennet Country* was published by Blackwells of Oxford in 1932. He and his wife voyaged along the navigation in 1919, even then not without difficulty, both mechanical and bureaucratic: 'It has cost me some weeks of negotiation with the railway company, and an initial outlay of twenty shillings to obtain a permit to enter the Kennet.' Swing-bridges 33 and 35 are hand-operated but take your windlass with you in case the locking bolts require a bit more than 'wrist action' to free them.

Halfway along the picturesquely wooded interlude between bridges 30 and 29, the Kennet leaves the canal and heads off in the direction of Aldermaston, being navigable, for those of a curious disposition, at least as far as Frouds Bridge Marina, if not Aldermaston Mill, which once received its grain by barge.

BUSINESS parks embower the A4, but the Kennet & Avon keeps its head down, unimpressed by technology, and marching past Aldermaston Wharf in its own silent protest at progress and man's inhumanity, not so much to man, as to the landscape.

Long before the era of the nuclear protest marches, the Great Western Railway inserted an arm off the main channel of the canal to facilitate interchange between rail and water. It paralleled the recently electrified railway for some distance but most of it was infilled at the outset of the World War II, and hastily erected offices sprang up to house staff evacuated from the GWR's Paddington headquarters.

For their part, the military authorities identified the K&A as a Blue Defence Line, pill boxes being installed at numerous locations. Fear makes fools of us all. Are we not equally irrational now in the face of terrorism and pandemics? According to Rolt: 'The last of the Kennet & Avon boatmen was dragged from retirement and put in charge of a leaking maintenance boat hauled by a broken-down horse led by a dim-witted youth'. Ere long, the vessel, overloaded by inexperienced squaddies, sank and put a summary end to the proceedings. Our old friend, the late George Behrend (author of that peerless railway book *Gone With Regret*) recalled

tank practice in the vicinity of the canal, and an altercation with a senior officer who refused to accept that the average K&A swingbridge was not necessarily designed to bear the weight of a tank.

Aldermaston Wharf lies a couple of miles north-east of Aldermaston itself. A bascule lift-bridge carries a busy road over the canal, operation by boaters being electronically prohibited during morning and evening rush-hour. The K&A's easternmost hire base adds to boat traffic.

On a hillside to the north, beyond the A4, Englefield House catches the eye from the pound between Tyle Mill and Sulhamstead locks. Researching this length one wintry day, we came upon horses splashing through floodwater in fields neighbouring the navigation like something out of the Camargue. Even in monochrome, and with foreshortened horizons, we could sense how beautiful the K&A could be at any time of the year, never mind its dragonfly-filled summers. Ufton Lock has disappeared. It was only shallow in any case, a mere 1ft 9ins, provided in the 1830s to give greater depth below Towney Lock. Towney was rebuilt as part of the restoration programme in 1974, and associated improvements rendered Ufton obsolete.

THE M4 motorway impinges briefly. You can marvel at its ugliness. One day it will be grass-grown, nothing is more certain. And then we will wonder at the romance of its heyday and form a preservation society to protect it.

As for the K&A you will be either conscious of its impending end or coming slowly to terms with its prosaic beginnings in a gravel pit flawed landscape. Keep the faith, back in 1919 Fred S. Thacker slaked his thirst at the Cunning Man (whose landlord didn't know the source of its name) discovered 'alluring lanes' leaving for Binfield, Grazeley and Shinfield and quickly learnt that a voyage along the Kennet 'is very delightful' - something of a British understatement.

Garston Lock, like Monkey Marsh (Map 17) is 'turf-sided' and one can't help thinking that the pillboxes overlooking it are there to protect it from that Fifth Columnist called Progress. At Bridge 17 the towpath changes sides and the National Cycle Route No.4 detours off to the south, passing former gravel workings now adopted by Theale Water Skiing Club.

Burghfield Lock - and, indeed, all the original twenty turf-sided locks between Reading and Newbury - originally dates from between 1715 and 1724, but was enlarged in the 1760s to accept the massive 'Newbury' barges which measured 19ft in the beam and 109ft in length and could carry a cargo of over a hundred tons. The lock chamber in use now dates from the early years of restoration and was ceremoniously opened by the Chairman of British Waterways in 1968.

Burghfield Mill, in common with Southcote to the east, was a typical Kennet watermill since converted for residential use. There were osier beds beside the canal between bridges 15 and 14. They were once harvested for basket making. Burghfield Island provides popular private moorings away from the main navigable channel under the aegis of the Burghfield Island Boat Club, entry being at the eastern end. Gravel extraction has largely ceased in the vicinity, but what is extracted now from the resultant lakes are huge carp weighing upwards of 40lbs.

Downstream of Southcote Lock the railway line from Reading to Basingstoke crosses the navigation. An important link between the midlands and the south, there are frequent passenger trains together with a considerable amount of container traffic making its way to and from Southampton Docks, making one wish there was still a residue of commercial traffic on the Kennet & Avon. Fobney Lock is overlooked by Reading's waterworks, pumping station and filter beds. A wildflower hay meadow is in the process of being re-created on Fobney Island.

Eating & Drinking

THE CUNNING MAN - canalside Bridge 14. Tel: 0118 959 8067. Large 'Vintage Inns' all-day canalside pub with garden. The unusual name derives from a local wizard. RG30 3RB

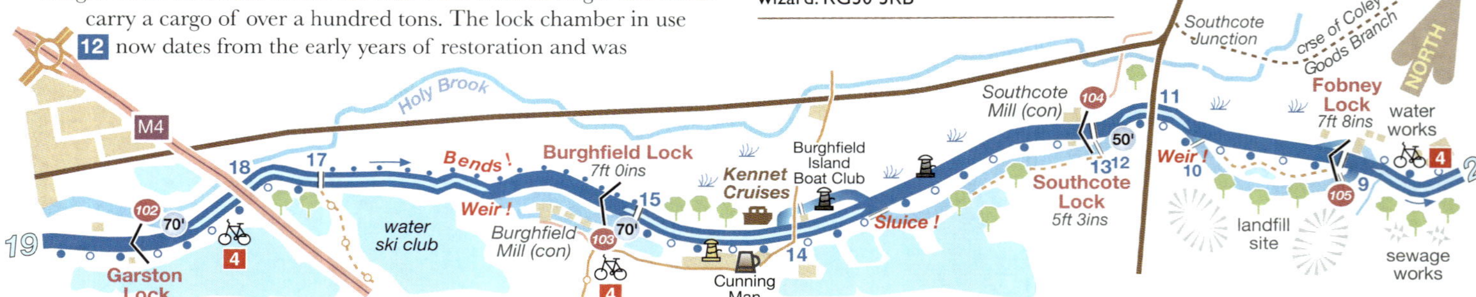

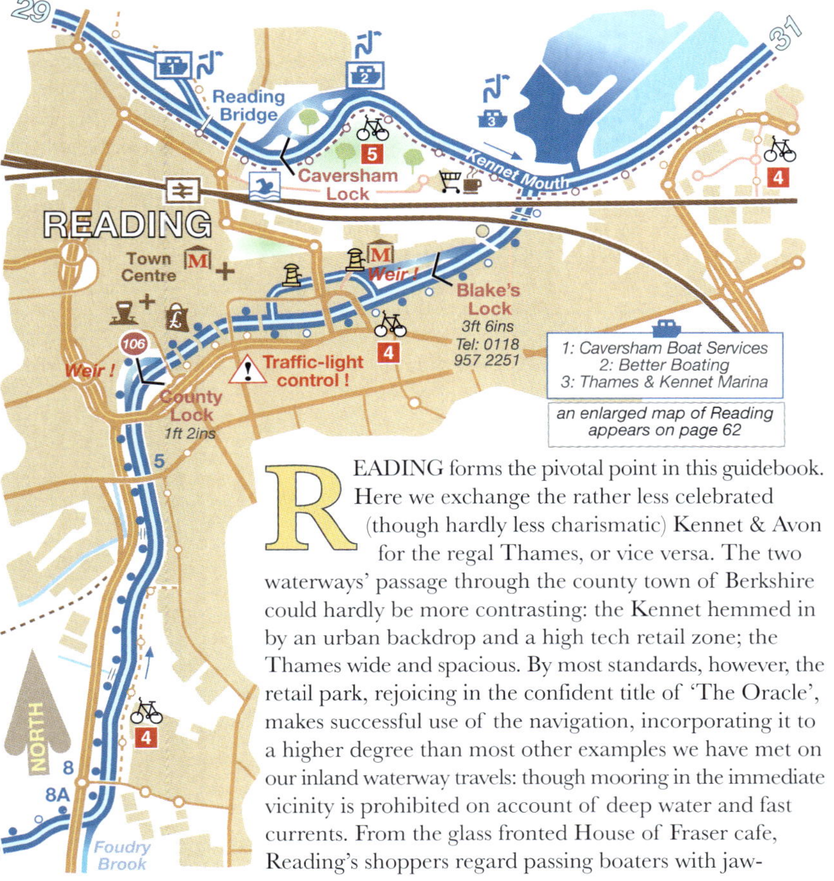

1: Caversham Boat Services
2: Better Boating
3: Thames & Kennet Marina

an enlarged map of Reading appears on page 62

READING forms the pivotal point in this guidebook. Here we exchange the rather less celebrated (though hardly less charismatic) Kennet & Avon for the regal Thames, or vice versa. The two waterways' passage through the county town of Berkshire could hardly be more contrasting: the Kennet hemmed in by an urban backdrop and a high tech retail zone; the Thames wide and spacious. By most standards, however, the retail park, rejoicing in the confident title of 'The Oracle', makes successful use of the navigation, incorporating it to a higher degree than most other examples we have met on our inland waterway travels: though mooring in the immediate vicinity is prohibited on account of deep water and fast currents. From the glass fronted House of Fraser cafe, Reading's shoppers regard passing boaters with jaw-dropping awe, perhaps in the sudden realisation that retail therapy can't compete with canal travel in the final analysis.

Eastbound, County Lock is the last under Canal & River Trust jurisdiction. The chamber was originally on the opposite bank of the river, but the GWR purloined Reading Basins to build their Central Goods Depot and the lock was re-sited in the process. Boaters proceed under traffic light control from here owing to the narrow nature of the channel ahead, one-way operation being the order of the day. The strength of the current increases: westbound you may notice that your boat is making heavy weather of its progress; eastbound, don't get carried away!

Simonds Brewery overlooked the Kennet (in the neighbourhood of what is now The Oracle) from 1789 onwards until the business was bought out by Courage in 1960 and, typically, closed a dozen years later. The navigation here was known as the 'Brewery Gut', and it was both deep and dangerous. As at Newbury, the absence of a towpath made difficult working practices for horse-drawn barges. At one point a line was attached to a pulley and the boat horse given a sharp smack on its hindquarters which had the effect of propelling the barge in to the bridgehole. Further on a long length of rope was floated down the navigation and attached to the barge, which had to be hauled a further two hundred yards from the bank. Ponder on these archaic working practices as you watch juggernauts unloading at the rear of the retail centre. Erected in 1787, High Bridge comes as an antidote to the almost surreal modernity of The Oracle.

A navigable backwater loops past Reading Gaol where Oscar Wilde was famously incarcerated for his sexual

continued overleaf:

continued from page 37:

proclivities. The Grade II listed gaol (designed by George Gilbert Scott) closed in 2013 and it's since seen use for art events, whilst the National Trust offer tours around it on selected dates. Visitor moorings are located by the ruins of Reading Abbey. Huntley & Palmer's biscuit factory overlooked this stretch of water, consisting in its heyday of a twenty-four acre site with six thousand employees producing over two hundred varieties of tinned biscuits. The new Prudential Building occupies much of this, a charmless landmark symbolic of industrial change. Up until the Second World War water transport was used both to bring flour in to Huntley & Palmers and take finished biscuits out, many destined for morale-boosting export to outposts of the Empire via London Docks. A dense network of terraced streets lay to the south of the Kennet to house H&P's workforce.

Blakes Lock (which belongs to the Environment Agency) is hand operated, but otherwise evinces all the characteristics of a Thames lock. Often the lock is to be found in 'self service' mode. Blake's Lock is said to be named after an 18th Century Mayor of Reading who opposed construction of the Kennet & Avon Canal - we can only be grateful he didn't get his way.

Railway bridges and a gasholder mark the confluence of the Kennet with the Thames. Prior to the Industrial Revolution the scene here must have been highly bucolic. The roving bridge dates from 1892, prior to which watermen and their horses were carried across the mouth of the river by ferry boat. Not the most romantic of backdrops, but the adrenalin is likely to be surging in any boater or walker making the transition - it always does at inland waterway junctions, whatever their nature.

Reading
Maps 21 & 30

Reading's skyline is dominated by The Blade, a 282 feet high tower block suggestive of a ship's prow. Squeezed between the Thames and the Kennet, Berkshire's county town exudes brash overtones of London, but manages to retain a provincial atmosphere. Broad Street, the handsome main thoroughfare embellished by terracotta and softened by plane trees, represents Reading's Edwardian zenith. We were saddened that Jackson's department store had closed since our previous visit. Its pneumatic 'cash railway' was perhaps the last in England. At an auction of the store's contents, it was purchased for a song by the man who had maintained it for over twenty years. Forbury Gardens (where the Maiwand Lion commemorates over three hundred members of the Berkshire Regiment lost in the Afghan War of the 1880s) and the nearby Abbey ruins are welcome oases of calm. Two churches deserve notice: St Laurence-in-Reading and St Mary the Virgin, the latter with a chequerboard tower of flint and limestone. In the 18th century Wiltshire stone was carried down the Kennet to build a crescent reminiscent of Bath on Queen's Road which runs parallel to the south of the canal east of High Bridge.

Eating & Drinking
BEL & THE DRAGON - Gasworks Road. Tel: 0118 951 5790. Charming contemporary restaurant & bar located alongside the Riverside Museum upstream of Blakes Lock. Sophisticated and secure 'fishbone' customer moorings lend it added appeal, and apparently the owners are keen boaters themselves. Sister establishments in Windsor and Cookham. RG1 3EQ
CARLUCCIO'S - Forbury Square. Tel: 0118 218 7089. Usually reliable Italian chain within easy reach of Kennet backwater moorings by Abbey. RG1 3EY
LONDON STREET BRASSERIE - London Street. High Bridge. Tel: 0118 950 5036. Stylish modern restaurant with terrace overlooking the navigation. RG1 4SE

Shopping
The Oracle offers 21st century shopping, but you know our sympathies lie elsewhere. Come with us to Union Street (off Broad Street and alias 'Smelly Alley') where a butcher, fishmonger and greengrocer ply their trade and you will have a clearer conscience. Farmers' Market on the first and third Saturdays of each month between 8.30am and 12pm. There are good moorings alongside a large Tesco (with a cafe) on the Thames upstream of its confluence with the Kennet.

Things to Do
RIVERSIDE MUSEUM - Gasworks Road. Tel: 0118 939 9800. Reading's social and industrial history housed in a former sewage pumping station. Wonderfully elegant gypsy vado built on Kennetside circa 1914 takes pride of place. RG1 3DH
MUSEUM OF READING - Town Hall. Tel: 0118 937 3400. Housed in Alfred Waterhouse's imposing town hall of 1875. Features a replica of the Bayeux Tapestry embroidered in Leek, Staffordshire in 1885. RG1 1QH
THAMES LIDO - Napier Road. Tel: 0118 207 0640. Magnificently restored outdoor swimming pool adjoining the Thames at King's Meadow. RG1 8FR

Connections
TRAINS - Great Western Railway services along the Thames and Kennet valleys. Tel: 0345 748 4950.

Bath Bottom Lock (Map 4)

Pulteney Weir, Bath (Map 4)

Avoncliffe Aqueduct (Map 5)

Bradford Lock (Map 5)

Caen Hill Locks (Map 8)

Newbury (Map 16)

44

High Bridge, Reading (Map 21)

Reading Bridge (Map 30)

Marlow Bridge (Map 34)

TOWN and Gown may define the City of Oxford's personality split, but the gulf is echoed by its canal and its river: the former self-effacing and humdrum, the latter exhibitionist and haughty.

Access between these contrasting inland waterways is by way of the Sheepwash Channel, spanned by the main railway line into Oxford from the north and overlooked by new housing. Upstream the Thames remains navigable as far as Lechlade, a delightful route covered effusively in the *Oxford & Grand Union Canal Companion*.

Via Osney Lock the Thames traverses the western periphery of Oxford, re-encountering the railway and passing beneath an ornate iron bridge which once carried a siding into a gasworks - only in Oxford could so elegant a structure be erected to carry so functional a transport facility. But for most residents and visitors the Thames at Oxford manifests itself most obviously at Folly Bridge where punts are available for hire and Salter's faded yet still elegant 'steamers' can still be taken throughout the summer season in stages downstream to Staines.

One wonders if it is the undergraduates or the tourists who take to punting nowadays, it seems too sentimental an activity for modern youth. Yet the college rowing clubs obviously continue to flourish, even if their stately barges have been for the most part replaced by club houses with a firm grasp of terra firma. With your gaze attracted by these sizeable

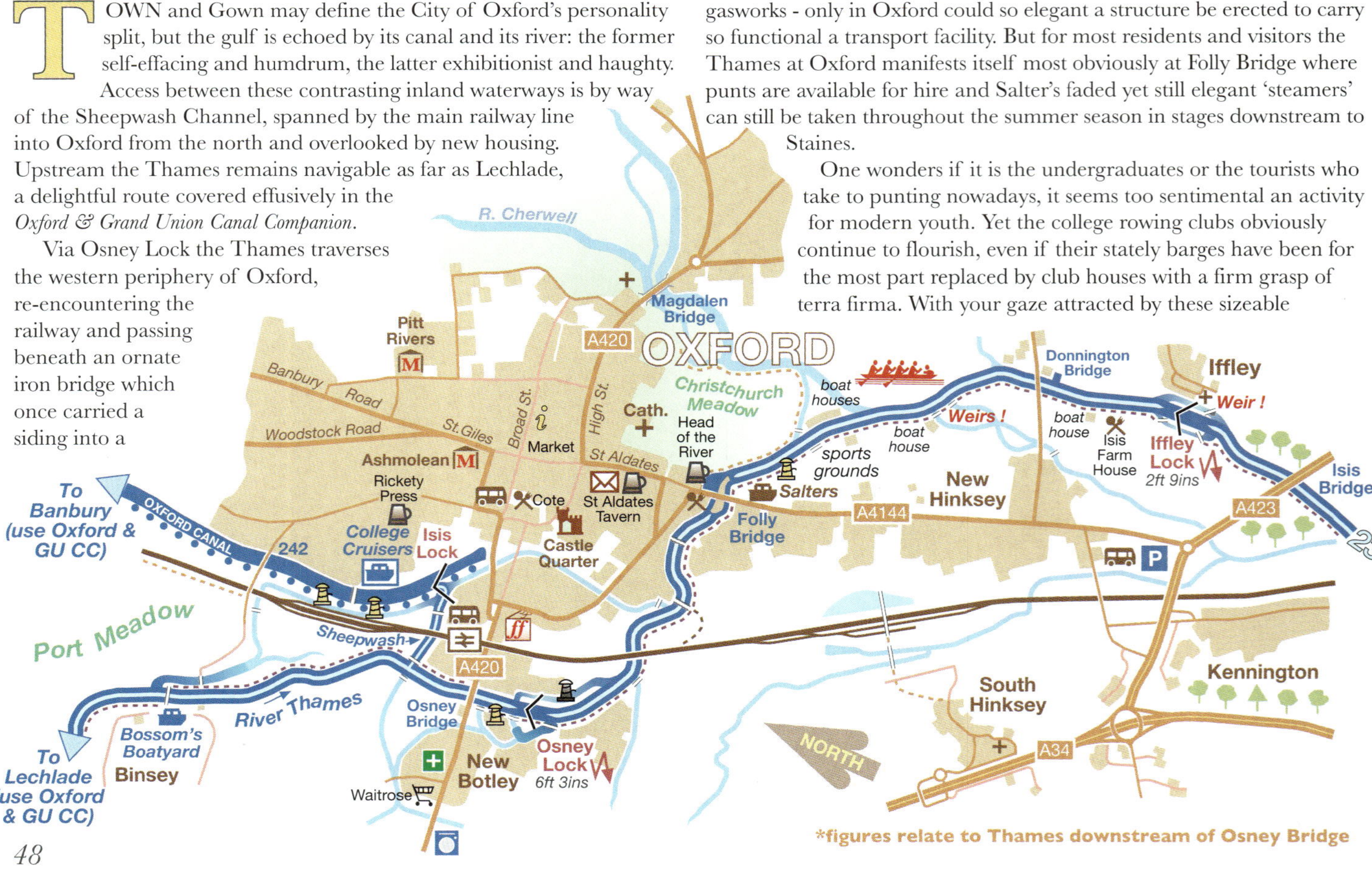

figures relate to Thames downstream of Osney Bridge

establishments you might miss the gentle ingress of the Cherwell, Oxford's most ethereal watercourse. More businesslike, the Thames negotiates the typically picturesque Iffley Lock, already establishing, for downstream newcomers, its capacity for escaping the less salubrious aspects of its mundane hinterland. Iffley's St Mary's was included in Simon Jenkins' book *England's Thousand Best Churches*. The equally appealing Old Parsonage, whose garden runs idyllically down to the Thames, is available for let through the estimable Landmark Trust.

Oxford   Map 22

However many times they are repeated, episodes of *Inspector Morse* seem to retain their charm, and much the same can be said of Colin Dexter's fictional detective's stamping ground; whilst adding water - in the shape of the Thames, the Cherwell, or the Oxford Canal - can only enhance the experience. Make no mistake, Oxford, one of the most beautiful medium-sized cities in the world, would lose half its magic without its waterways.

Eating & Drinking

COTE BRASSERIE - George Street. Tel: 01865 251992. Reliable chain open 8am (9am Sat & Sun). OX1 2BE

THE FOLLY - Folly Bridge. Tel: 01865 201293. Waterside (literally) cafe/restaurant. OX1 4JU

GEORGINA'S - Covered Market. Tel: 01865 249527. Iconic first floor cafe open 8am-5pm ex Sun. Still cosy after all these years! OX1 3DY

HEAD OF THE RIVER - Folly Bridge. Tel: 01865 721600. Popular Fuller's inn/hotel. OX1 4LB

ISIS FARMHOUSE - riverside above Iffley Lock. Tel: 01865 243854. Isolated yet popular riverside cafe/pub. Home made food and locally brewed ales. OX4 4EL

KING'S ARMS - Sandford Lock (Map 23). Tel: 01865 777095. Chef & Brewer pub restaurant. OX4 4YB

THE NOSEBAG - St Michael's Street. Tel: 01865 721033. Long-established wholefood/vegetarian cafe restaurant. Open from 9.30am daily. OX1 2DU

THE RICKETY PRESS - Cranham Street, Jericho. Tel: 01865 424851. Open from noon daily. OX2 6DE

ST ALDATES TAVERN - St Aldates. Tel: 01865 241185. *Good Beer Guide* listed city pub offering a wide choice of beer and food. Opens 11.30am. OX1 1BU

Shopping

Drawing on a wide range of custom and taste, Oxford's shops are inspired to an admirable eclecticism. The Covered Market (off High Street) hosts the most wonderful cross-section of retailers and those who have travelled the length and breadth of this guide from Bristol will find a resemblance to the market there. As befits a seat of learning, there are many good bookshops, not least Blackwell's on The Broad.

Things to Do

OXFORD VISITOR INFORMATION CENTRE - Broad Street. Tel: 01865 686430. OX1 3AS

ASHMOLEAN MUSEUM - Beaumont Street. Tel: 01865 278000. Britain's oldest public museum displaying European, Egyptian and Near Eastern antiquities. Closed Mondays. Nice rooftop restaurant. OX1 2PH

CARFAX TOWER - Carfax. 99 steps to heaven for a bird's eye view of the city of dreaming spires.

CITY SIGHTSEEING - open top bus rides with running commentary. Regular departures from the railway station and city centre stops.

MUSEUM OF OXFORD - St Aldates. Tel: 01865 252334. Local history made good. OX1 1BX

OXFORD CASTLE & PRISON - New Road. Tel: 01865 260666. Award-winning visitor attraction. OX1 1AY

PITT RIVERS MUSEUM - South Parks Road. Tel: 01865 613000. Anthropology and archaeology. OX1 3PP

PUNT HIRE - Oxford's most traditional means of seduction (and indeed various other types of self-propelled craft) can be hired from boat houses at Folly Bridge (Tel: 01865 243421 - OX1 4LA) on the Thames and Magdalen Bridge (Tel: 01865 202643 - OX1 4AX) on the Cherwell.

COLLEGES - over thirty colleges make up Oxford University. Many of them are world famous such as Balliol and Merton which are both of 13th century origin; Magdalen (pronounced 'Maudlin') which dates from 1458; and Christ Church founded in 1525 by Cardinal Wolsey. The general (less well-educated) public may look around most of them in the afternoons.

OPEN SPACES - much of Oxford's charm rests in the proliferation of green spaces, the city's lungs. These include: The Parks, Christ Church Meadow and Port Meadow. A stroll - or a picnic - on any of them comes as a refreshing experience after the hurly-burly of the main thoroughfares and helps put Oxford in the context of its riverside setting.

Connections

TRAINS - services along the Thames Valley to/from Reading and London and connections to/from the midlands and the north. Tel: 0345 748 4950.

BUSES - Oxford Bus Company services X3 and X13 operate at frequent intervals from the railway station forecourt and/or St Aldates to/from Abingdon making them ideal for one-way walks along the Thames Path. Ditto Thames Travel X2. Tel: 0871 200 2233.

PERHAPS even the Thames itself would admit to being at its most lacklustre between Iffley and Abingdon. In the reach below Sandford Lock especially it is characterised by accompanying scrubland and a plethora of electricity pylons. But these are minor lapses in concentration and quickly forgiven. Elsewhere on this stretch there is much to look out for and muse over. Kennington Railway Bridge carries the rump of the old line via Thame to Princes Risborough, of which there are aspirations for re-opening as far as Oxford Business Park. Meanwhile, it's used by goods trains bearing Minis from the motor works in nearby Cowley. Another victim of time's remorseless passage has been the paper mill at Sandford Lock. Narrowboats used to bring coal down from the Warwickshire coalfield to feed its hungry furnaces. Closed in 1982, its former site is inevitably occupied by housing now, but you may care to know that William Stroudley, the locomotive engineer, was born in Sandford and apprenticed at the mill before joining the railways.

Sandford, with an almost nine foot fall, is the deepest lock upstream of Teddington. Its origins can be traced back to 1632, but the lock-keeper's cottage dates from 1914. Michael Llewelyn Davies - J. M. Barrie's ward, and inspiration for *Peter Pan* - drowned, along with a fellow undergraduate, at Sandford in 1921 in dubious circumstances. The unofficial 1943 Boat Race was held on a course between the tail of Sandford Lock and Radley College boathouse - Oxford won by two-thirds of a length! The following year the contest took place on the Great Ouse at Littleport, downstream of Ely: ditto 2021! A vibrant local produce market is held in Sandford's village hall on Saturday mornings; the aroma of bacon sandwiches wafts down to the river!

Nuneham House overlooks the river and in its gracious grounds stands the Carfax Conduit, an artefact pertaining to Oxford's 17th century water supply rendered redundant by the widening of High Street in 1787. Not a great deal can be seen from the river of the house itself (in which Victoria and Albert honeymooned in 1841) but the grounds are the work of no lesser a gardener than 'Capability' Brown. Charles Dodgson (aka Lewis Carroll) used to row Alice Liddell down to Nuneham as an alternative to their more regular forays upstream to Godstow. Lock Wood Island recalls the existence of a lock at this point which ceased being used around 1800, at which time the channel changed from the east side to the west.

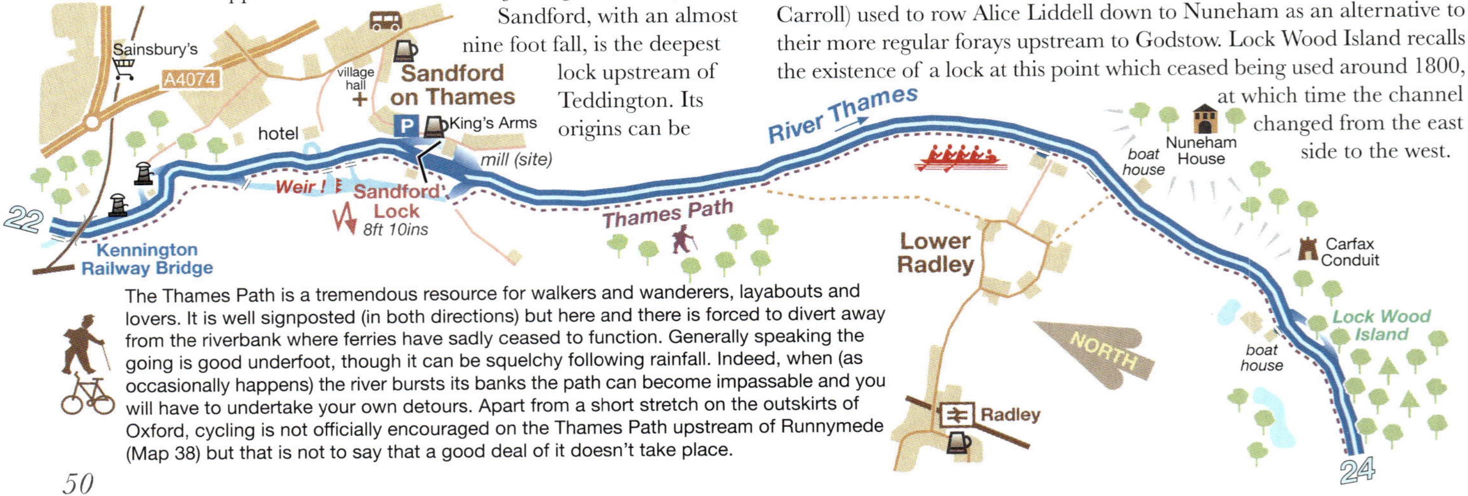

The Thames Path is a tremendous resource for walkers and wanderers, layabouts and lovers. It is well signposted (in both directions) but here and there is forced to divert away from the riverbank where ferries have sadly ceased to function. Generally speaking the going is good underfoot, though it can be squelchy following rainfall. Indeed, when (as occasionally happens) the river bursts its banks the path can become impassable and you will have to undertake your own detours. Apart from a short stretch on the outskirts of Oxford, cycling is not officially encouraged on the Thames Path upstream of Runnymede (Map 38) but that is not to say that a good deal of it doesn't take place.

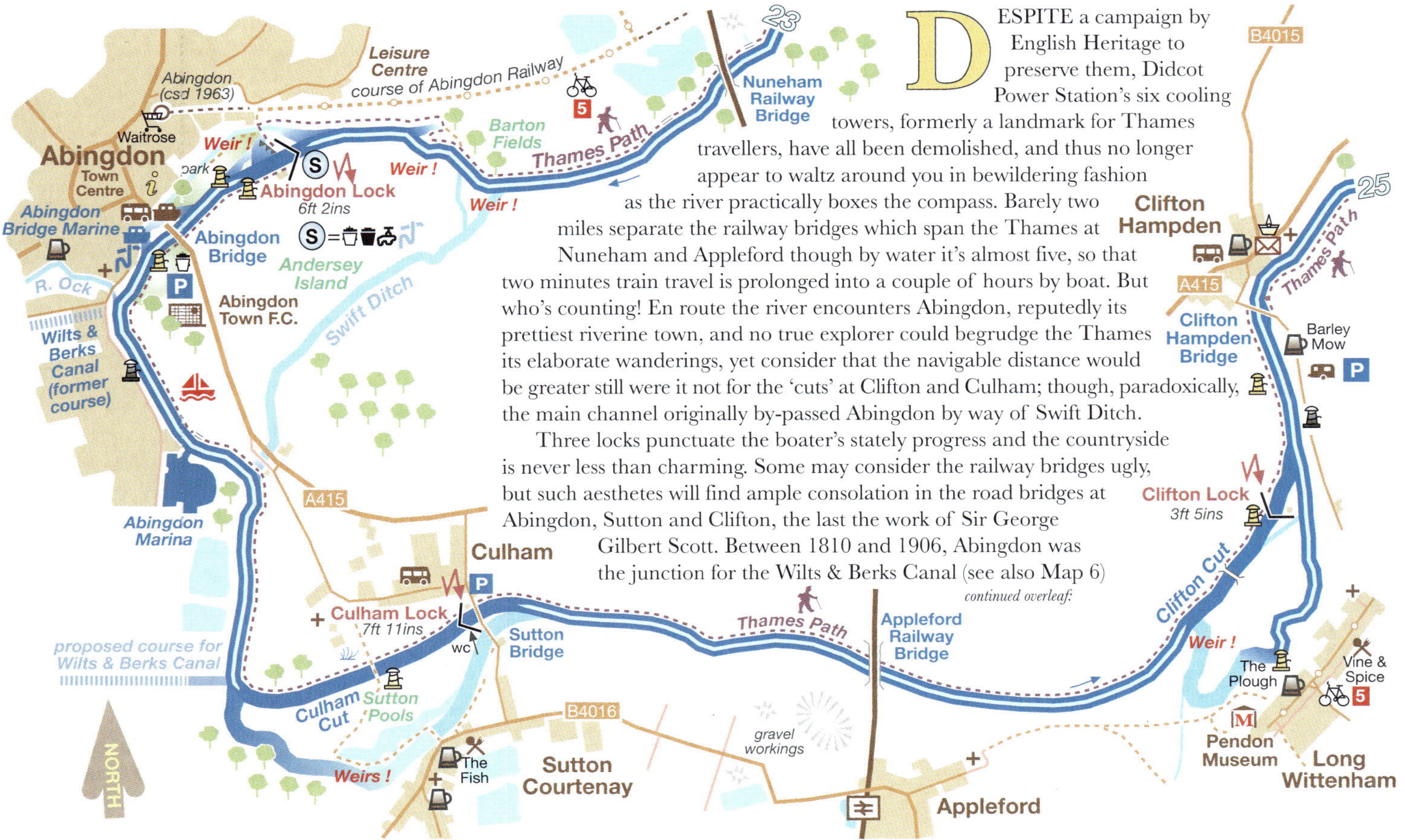

DESPITE a campaign by English Heritage to preserve them, Didcot Power Station's six cooling towers, formerly a landmark for Thames travellers, have all been demolished, and thus no longer appear to waltz around you in bewildering fashion as the river practically boxes the compass. Barely two miles separate the railway bridges which span the Thames at Nuneham and Appleford though by water it's almost five, so that two minutes train travel is prolonged into a couple of hours by boat. But who's counting! En route the river encounters Abingdon, reputedly its prettiest riverine town, and no true explorer could begrudge the Thames its elaborate wanderings, yet consider that the navigable distance would be greater still were it not for the 'cuts' at Clifton and Culham; though, paradoxically, the main channel originally by-passed Abingdon by way of Swift Ditch.

Three locks punctuate the boater's stately progress and the countryside is never less than charming. Some may consider the railway bridges ugly, but such aesthetes will find ample consolation in the road bridges at Abingdon, Sutton and Clifton, the last the work of Sir George Gilbert Scott. Between 1810 and 1906, Abingdon was the junction for the Wilts & Berks Canal (see also Map 6)

for details of facilities at Abingdon turn to page 52; Sutton Courtenay, Clifton Hampden and Long Wittenham turn to page 53

continued from page 51:

agricultural produce; although, ironically, it did prove useful in the movement of materials for construction of the Great Western Railway through the Vale of the White Horse. Unlike the Kennet & Avon, it was a narrowbeam canal, and this restriction certainly did it no favours with the advent of the Railway Age. Trade at the Abingdon end had all but evaporated in the 1880s and there is virtually no trace of the canal's junction with the Thames other than a slight indentation in the retaining wall above Wilsham Road, close to where the River Ock (Middle English for salmon) joins the main river beneath a little iron bridge bearing the misleading inscription: 'Wilts & Berks Canal 1824'. Abingdon might have become an inland waterway crossroads if the plan for a canal to Aylesbury had ever come to fruition. The enthusiastic Wilts & Berks Canal Trust continue to campaign for restoration of the canal, and have unveiled the beginnings of a new linking section to the south of Abingdon Marina.

Clifton Cut dates from 1822, and Culham Cut from 1809. Prior to their construction trade was hampered by flash locks and the use of the river by a watermill at Sutton Courtenay. Swift Ditch probably represented the original course of the river before Abingdon's monks diverted the channel past their abbey. In the 17th century Swift Ditch regained its importance as the main line of navigation and featured one of the earliest pound-locks in England. Around 1790, with the construction of a lock at Abingdon, Swift Ditch lost its status and became a backwater once again.

Appleford Railway Bridge dates from 1843 and its construction led to much debate between the Thames Commissioners and the Great Western Railway whose line approached the river from either direction on low-lying ground. A high bridge to facilitate the passage of masted vessels would have necessitated lengthy approach embankments which would have been detrimental to high speed running. The railway builders appear to have had things their way, for the bow span girder bridge stands only thirteen feet above water, the third lowest crossing on the whole river below Oxford.

Abingdon
Map 30

Excellent municipal moorings - provided, what's more, free of charge - can only add to the popularity of what locals will proudly tell you is 'the oldest town in Britain', and Abingdon is indeed an engaging town full of architectural, cultural and historical surprises. Pearsons would not be Pearsons, though, if we did not take umbrage at Abingdon's post 1974 transfer from Berkshire to Oxfordshire, the crass meddling of politicians and bureaucrats overturning the stabilities of centuries. And there have been two well known commercial casualties - MG motor cars and the Morland brewery. That off our chests, we commend Abingdon to you and suggest that you see the remains of the Abbey, St Helen's high-spired, flying-buttressed church, and the amazing County Hall, a Wren-like building which has not unreasonably been declared 'the grandest town hall in England'.

Eating & Drinking
ASK - The Square. Tel: 01235 529699. Italian chain housed in old Congregational Chapel. OX14 5SZ
BREWERY TAP - Ock Street. Tel: 01235 521655. *Good Beer Guide* listed, stone-floored, wood-panelled pub. Erstwhile 'tap' of Morland Brewery. OX14 5BZ
BROAD FACE - Bridge Street. Tel: 01235 538612. Stylish, *Good Beer Guide* listed pub open 11am (11.30 Sun). OX14 3HR
LIMONCELLO - Ock Street. Tel: 01235 530900. Homely Italian. Dinner from 6pm ex Sun. OX14 5AL
MEZZEH HOUSE - The Square. Tel: 01235 533551. Lebanese restaurant open Mon-Sat for lunch and dinner (from 5pm) and Sunday from 6pm. OX14 5AR
NAG'S HEAD - The Bridge. Tel: 01235 524516. *GBG* listed riverside pub open from 11am daily (noon Sun). Up to eight real ales on tap. Al fresco dining riverside throughout the summer months. OX14 3HX

Shopping
A good place to shop, if not quite so relaxed as Wallingford. A branch of Waitrose occupies the site of the old railway station, erstwhile terminus of the line from Radley. Retail market on Monday, and Farmers' Market on the 3rd Friday in the month.

Things to Do
VISITOR INFORMATION CENTRE - Bridge Street. Tel: 01235 522711. 9.30am-3pm ex Sun. OX14 3HU
ABINGDON MUSEUM - County Hall, Market Place. Tel: 01235 523703. Worth visiting just to be in the beautiful building which houses it. OX14 3HG

Connections
BUSES - services X2, X3*, X13 & X32 run frequently to/from Abingdon and Oxford city centre (St Aldates) and railway station*. Services X2, X32 and 33 operate southwards to Didcot Parkway railway station. Tel: 0871 200 2233.

Clifton Hampden Map 30

"Self-consciously picturesque" avowed John Piper in his 1938 *Shell Guide to Oxfordshire*, and you can still see what he meant. Sergeant William Dykes, who accidentally began the Battle of Waterloo, is buried in the churchyard. Good little post office stores.

Eating & Drinking

BARLEY MOW - riverside. Tel: 01865 407847. This famous and popular inn ('the quaintest, most old-world inn up the river' according to JKJ) is now part of the Chef & Brewer chain. MG used to use its picturesque appearance as a backdrop for their publicity shots. Moorings opposite. OX14 3EH

Long Wittenham Map 30

Backwaters always beguile, and moorings to the rear of The Plough offer every inducement to turn temporarily away from the main channel to explore the low-lying village of Long Wittenham. The predominantly Early English church is very pretty. Robert Gibbings, the engraver, and author of *Sweet Thames Run Softly* and its elegiac sequel *Till I End My Song* - who spent his last years in Long Wittenham - is buried in the graveyard. Another erstwhile resident of renown and vision was Roye England the model maker and founder of the Pendon Museum who arrived here n 1954 and converted the old Three Poplars pub into a Youth Hostel.

Eating & Drinking

THE PLOUGH - High Street. Tel: 01865 407738. *Good Beer Guide* listed village pub with a long garden leading down to the riverbank where there is good decking for mooring a couple of boats. Accommodation, food and a fine choice of real ales. OX14 4QH
VINE & SPICE - High Street. Tel: 01865 409900. Asian cuisine in delightful surroundings. OX14 4QH

Things to Do

PENDON MUSEUM - Tel: 01865 407365. 'Museum' is a misnomer, Pendon houses an extraordinary 1:76 model of the Vale of the White Horse c1930s which has taken the best part of fifty years to build and work continues. Other exhibits include a railway running at the edge of Dartmoor, a sea wall scene based on Teignmouth in Devon, and John Ahern's ground breaking Madder Valley Railway first constructed in the 1930s which runs from Gammon End through Much Madder to Madderport. Spellbinding and absolutely not to be missed! Cafe and shop. Open 2-5pm Sats and Suns and also Weds in July and August. OX14 4QD

Connections

TRAINS - Appleford (a pleasant mile's walk by field paths to the west) is reasonably well-served by Great Western Railway stopping services. Tel: 0345 748 4950.

Sutton Courtenay Map 30

An embarrassment of fine buildings characterises this quiet village on ostensibly unnavigable backwaters. Unfortunately it is some distance on foot from the nearest moorings on Culham Reach. A mere detail, which should not dissuade you from visiting Sutton, the pools are utterly picturesque and Eric Blair (aka George Orwell) is buried towards the bottom right corner of the churchyard which also includes the grave of the Liberal P.M. Asquith whose great-granddaughter is the actress Helena Bonham Carter.

Eating & Drinking

THE FISH - Appleford Road. Tel: 01235 848242. Fine restaurant/bar run by two Frenchmen. Open daily ex Monday, and Sunday evenings. OX14 4NQ

Connections

BUSES - Thames Travel 33 to/from Didcot and Abingdon hourly. Tel: 0871 200 2233.

Dorchester Map 31

Not to be confused with Dorset's rather better known Dorchester deep in the heart of Thomas Hardy country, Dorchester-on-Thames (and surely that should be Dorchester-on-*Thame*) is a gloriously sleepy place, by-passed (relatively recently) by the main road and by-passed, evidently, by time itself. Even hazy historians will realise, given the second syllable of its name, that it boasts Roman origins. Accessible from informal moorings above or below Day's Lock - from which a footpath leads across the prehistoric mounds of the Dyke Hills - the centre is dominated by a Decorated Abbey approached through a Butterfield lych gate and justly renowned for its astonishing Jesse window. Dorchester is often used for filming *Midsomer Murders*, so brace yourself for a high body count.

Eating & Drinking

FLEUR DE LYS - High Street. Tel: 01865 661865. 16th century pub, restaurant and hotel. OX10 7HH
GEORGE HOTEL - High Street. Tel: 01865 340404. Originally a coaching inn which can trace its history back to the 15th century. Nice choice of real ales. OX10 7HH
LILY'S - High Street. Tel: 01865 340900. Family run tea room and farm shop (closed Tuesdays). OX10 7HN
Teas often also available at The Abbey.

Shopping

Centre for antiques, Dorchester's practical shopping is restricted to a Co-op convenience store.

Things to Do

ABBEY MUSEUM - Tel: 01865 340007. Museum devoted to local history and the abbey. Of particular interest is a 16th century schoolroom displaying education through the ages. There is also a cloister gallery. Open Wed-Sun Easter-September 2pm-5pm. OX10 7HH

25 RIVER THAMES Shillingford 5mls/11k/2hrs

IN some circles - albeit ever decreasing ones - the Thames above its confluence with the confusingly named Thame is known as Isis. This River Thame, navigable (despite appearances) as far as Dorchester by the intrepid crews of diminutive vessels, rises to the east of Aylesbury, close to the Grand Union Canal. Its name derives from an eponymous market town on the north-eastern border of Oxfordshire notable in that the eccentric restaurateur John Fothergill once kept the Spread Eagle there.

John Masefield (*Sea Fever*, *The Box of Delights*) lived beside the river at Burcot for many years. Hereabouts the Thames is dominated visually by the Sinodun Hills, alias Wittenham Clumps; little more than three hundred feet above sea level, though positively mountainous in the context of the Thames flood plain. The artist Paul Nash was captivated by these scenes, especially under moonlight, and produced several paintings of them

it your business to explore Little Wittenham Nature Reserve, lovingly tended by the Earth Trust, who have a visitor centre (Tel: 01865 407792 - OX14 4QZ) at Little Wittenham. Waymarked trails lead through the woods or to the top of Round Hill and Castle Hill from which there are prodigious views and remnants of Iron Age fortifications. From these superior viewpoints more visual sense can be made of the Dyke Hills on the east bank of the river above Day's Lock.

Shillingford Bridge, graceful, dating from 1827 and marking the halfway point between Reading and Oxford, is overlooked by an hotel with a riverside open air swimming pool. The Irish poet Yeats lived briefly in Shillingford during 1921; whilst, if his mother was to be believed, Vivian Stanshall of the Bonzo Dog Doo-Dah Band was born here in 1943, though his father always maintained it was Walthamstow!

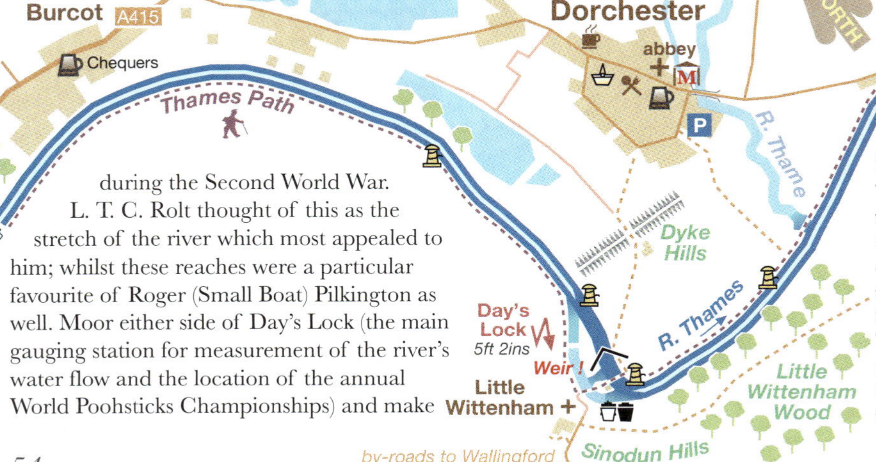

for details of facilities at Dorchester turn back to page 53

THE Thames appears to move at a more sedate pace than its 21st century hinterland. Journeying on or beside it offers the opportunity to fall back through the years to what we now perceive as a gentler era of canvassed camping skiffs and meadowland picnics. Solely a proliferation of abandoned pill boxes introduces a sense of unease. You wonder what were they designed to protect, and the answer is RAF Benson, closely associated with de Havilland 'Mosquitos'. In the Second World War these aircraft had sufficient range to reach the Balkans, and Benson was home of the Photographic Reconnaissance Unit. Nowadays it remains a vibrant base for Puma HC2 helicopters. Benson Lock cottage is dated 1913, before the concept of world wars existed at all. Flood level plaques adorn its walls, some anachronistically pre-dating it. The Thames Path changes banks, and the walker enjoys an entertaining interlude bridging the lengthy weir. Jethro Tull - the inventor of the horse-drawn seed drill, as opposed to the 1960s rock band - lived in Crowmarsh Gifford between 1700 and 1710 - see also Map 28.

Wallingford Bridge boasts seventeen arches, though only five span the river. The bridge is overlooked by the slender open spire of St Peter's Church, and a converted warehouse recalls the days when Wallingford relied more fully on the river for its commerce than it does now. Altogether a pleasingly mellow scene, and formal moorings (provided on either bank upstream of the bridge) enable boaters to pause awhile and soak it up; though here - ignoring Abingdon's munificent lead - a charge is levied overnight.

Though their attitude to boaters differs, Wallingford and Abingdon were firmly against the advent of the Railway Age, both spurning Brunelian advances to bring the Great Western Railway to their doorstep. The entrenched self-interest of river traders may have had a bearing on this hostility, but it did result in isolation from the march of 19th century commerce and industry. Eventually both towns lowered their guard and linked themselves optimistically to the main line, but too late for their shortlived branches - closed to passengers respectively in 1959 and 1963 - to rouse their

continued overleaf:

The Thames Path detours briefly away from the river on two occasions. At Benson take care passing through the boatyard then follow the lane before reaching the footpath down to the weir. By Wallingford Bridge the path leaves the river, following alleyways and side-streets before regaining the river by the Oxford University Boat Club's impressive premises.

for details of facilities at Benson and Wallingford turn to page 72

continued from page 55:

towns out of their historic torpor.

Half a mile downstream of Wallingford Bridge lay Wallingford, or more properly, Chalmore Hole Lock. It was deemed superfluous in 1883, just in time for it to be included as a humorous aside in *Three Men In A Boat*.

South of Winterbrook Bridge, which carries Wallingford by-pass across the Thames, the Thames Path is joined by The Ridgeway, the two National Trails hugging their respective riverbanks as far as Streatley. The Ridgeway runs from Avebury in Wiltshire to Ivinghoe Beacon in Hertfordshire, a distance of eighty-five miles. This is red kite country, so the large bird wheeling above you is not necessarily the increasingly ubiquitous buzzard.

Benson
Map 26

Also occasionally known as Bensington, Benson is chiefly known for its RAF base these days, though a couple of centuries ago it was an important staging post for coaches on the Oxford to Henley run. The centre of the village lies across the busy A4074 whose motorists defy the Geneva Convention.

Eating & Drinking
THE WATERFRONT - Benson Waterfront. Tel: 01491 833732. Versatile riverside cafe bar & bistro with heated terrace overlooking the water. OX10 6SJ
THE VILLAGE PLAICE - High Street. Tel: 01491 826331. Fish & chips lunch and evening ex Sundays. OX10 6RP *There are also two pubs in the village and an Indian take-away - Tel: 01491 833326/7.*

Shopping
You'll have to walk into the village centre (taking care of the traffic) where you'll find a small Co-op supermarket, butcher, grocer, and pharmacy.

Connections
BUSES - 'River Rapids' X39/40 run half-hourly Mon-Sat, hourly Sun to/from Oxford, Wallingford and Reading. Tel: 0871 200 2233.

Wallingford
Map 26

The prehistoric origins of 'Walling Ford' are self explanatory. Alfred the Great fortified the town against the Danes and William the Conqueror erected a castle here. It dominated the town for five hundred years and in the 12th century supported Queen Matilda against King Stephen. When decay set in, Henry VIII ordered much of its timber and lead to be shipped downstream for enlarging Windsor Castle. Overlooking the river bridge, St Peter's 18th century church replaced one which Cromwell's soldiery had 'knocked about a bit'. Within lies the tomb of Sir William Blackstone (1723-80) on whose *Commentaries on the Laws of England* the American Constitution was based, but perhaps he is best remembered for his dictum that 'it is better that ten guilty men go free than one innocent man suffer'. St Peter's is cared for by the Churches Conservation Trust (as are the charming churches at Nuneham Murren and Mongewell) and the key (if locked) is obtainable from the Tourist Information Centre. Wallingford's other famous resident was Agatha Christie, who lived at Winterbrook House on the outskirts of the town for forty years. Wallingford doubles as Causton, home to Inspector Barnaby of *Midsomer Murders* fame.

Eating & Drinking
AVANTI - High Street. Tel: 01491 835500. Genuinely atmospheric Italian. OX10 0BW
BEAN & BREW - St Mary's Street. Tel: 01491 520685. Excellent coffee house and tea room. OX10 0EL
THE BOAT HOUSE - High Street Tel: 01491 834100. Comfortable riverside bar/restaurant. OX10 0BJ
LE CLOS - St Mary's Street. Tel: 01491 598151. Convivial wine bar. OX10 0EL
OLD POST OFFICE - St Martin's Street. Tel: 01491 836068. Open from 10am Wed-Sun. OX10 0AA

Shopping
Wallingford is a pleasant place to shop with a Waitrose supermarket well-integrated into the centre of town. Wallingford Bookshop and Wallingford Butchers - both situated on St Martin's Street - are not to be confused; the latter are also fishmongers. Friday is market day, whilst on 1st & 5th Saturdays and 3rd Tuesdays there's a Farmers'/Craft market.

Things to Do
TOURIST INFORMATION CENTRE - Market Sq. Tel: 01491 826972. OX10 0EG
WALLINGFORD MUSEUM - High Street. Tel: 01491 835065. Local history exhibitions including: the castle; transport routes; Agatha Christie and Midsomer Murders. Open Mar-Nov, Tue-Fri afternoons, Saturdays 10.30-5pm. Also Sundays Jun & Aug. OX10 0DB
CHOLSEY & WALLINGFORD RAILWAY - Tel: 01491 835067. Nostalgic rides along the former branch line from Cholsey. A pair of the resident diesel locomotives used to work for Guinness at Park Royal. OX10 9GQ

Connections
BUSES - Thames Travel service X38 links Wallingford with Henley on Thames; X2 runs to/from the railhead at Didcot; 'River Rapids' X39/40 operate to/fro Reading and Oxford. Going Forward service 134 runs to/from Goring Mon-Sat. Tel: 0871 200 2233.
TAXIS - Wally. Tel: 01491 260029.

NEVER a dull moment as the Thames flows purposefully through the Goring Gap, an Ice Age leftover between the Berkshire Downs and The Chilterns. Walkers have to decide which pathway suits them best: the Thames Path upstream of Streatley hugging the west bank, The Ridgeway the east. Inevitably, the old ferries at Little Stoke and Moulsford no longer function, so crossing the river and combining the paths into circular walks is not a ready option. Why was it so easy to let ferry rights lapse when they were an essential component of public rights of way? Moulsford Railway Bridge was originally the work of Isambard Kingdom Brunel and as such dates from 1840. When the line was quadrupled fifty years later, a second span was added on the downstream side, linked to the older bridge by curious little cross arches.

Moulsford ferry was immortalised anonymously by H. G. Wells in his delightful novel *The History of Mr. Polly*, which, by virtue of the chapter called 'The Potwell Inn' alone, deserves its niche in the pantheon of Thames inspired literature. Apparently Wells stayed at the Beetle & Wedge Inn whilst engaged on the book. Alfred Polly, who found convivial employment as the ferryman, would not recognise the inn now, for it has become smart and orientated in the general direction of fine cuisine, but his memory lingers affectionately on in the minds of ferry enthusiasts.

Cleeve Lock, the shallowest on the Thames, is backed by a maze of islets and backwaters. The pound between the locks at Goring and Cleeve is the shortest on the river, whilst, strangely, that between Cleeve and Benson is the lengthiest. David Blagrove was a relief keeper at Goring Lock in the early 1960s, and describes his work here - and at the next three locks downstream - in his book *The Quiet Waters By*. Goring Bridge carries both The Ridgeway and the Thames Path across the river, its length necessitated by the weir channel and the millstream, a quintessential Thames scene of great charm. Oscar Wilde once lived in the old Ferry Cottage which later became the home of 'Bomber Harris', the controversial architect of Britain's blanket bombing raids on Germany.

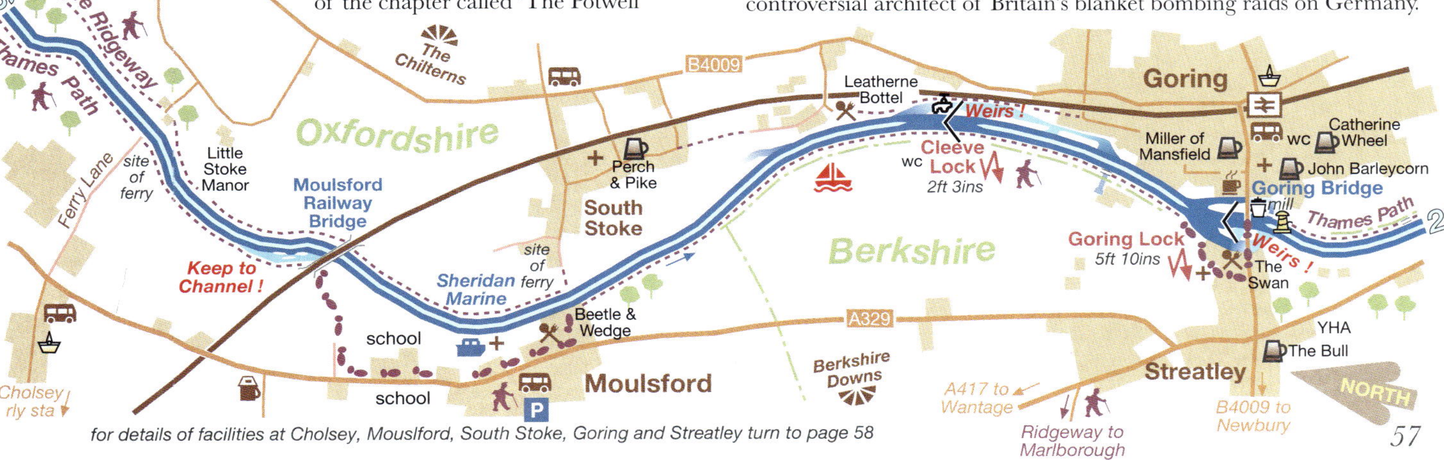

for details of facilities at Cholsey, Mouslford, South Stoke, Goring and Streatley turn to page 58

Goring Map 27

Perhaps the quintessential Thameside village, Goring has been the scene of an annual regatta since 1887. Good moorings below the bridge offer easy access to quaint streets where the use of flint and timber is prevalent. The Norman church boasts one of the oldest bells in Britain. Walkers on The Ridgeway and Thames Path may doff their hats to each other as they cross the river.

Eating & Drinking

JOHN BARLEYCORN - Manor Road. Tel: 01491 872509. Comfortable pub offering Brakspear ales, food & accommodation. RG8 9DP

CATHERINE WHEEL - Station Road. Tel: 01491 872379. Traditional pub offering a good choice of food including take-aways. RG8 9HB

LEATHERNE BOTTEL - Cleeve. Tel: 01491 872667. Don Giovanni's Italian restaurant in gorgeous riverside setting upstream of Cleeve Lock. RG8 0HS

MASOOM'S - High Street. Tel: 01491 875078. Tandoori restaurant & take-away. RG8 9AT

THE MILLER OF MANSFIELD - High Street. Tel: 01491 872829. 18th century coaching inn offering bar/restaurant food and accommodation. RG8 9AW

PIERREPONTS - Bridge Approach. Tel: 01491 874464. Marvellous cafe at the foot of the bridge. Open Tue-Sat 8am-5pm. Deli too. RG8 9AB

Shopping

Goring is a good spot to lay on stores without having to fight your way through the crowds. Facilities include a McColl's convenience store (with PO), butcher, pharmacist, and gift shop. But best of all is The Goring Grocer (Tel: 01491 875609 - RG8 9AR) a cornucopia of splendid foodstuffs. New Tesco Express up by the railway station.

Connections

TRAINS - Great Western Railway services to/from Paddington and Didcot usefully calling at Pangbourne and Cholsey for walkers. Tel: 0345 748 4950. BUSES - Going Forward service 134 provides a useful (ex Sun) link with Wallingford. Tel: 0871 200 2233. TAXIS - Murdoch's. Tel: 01491 872029.

Streatley Map 27

Odd how each river crossing throws up neighbouring communities where the economy of one has thrived at the expense of the others. In this case Streatley is the shy, retiring type and many would remark all the more appealing for it, and indeed there are some charming brick buildings in the vernacular Thames Valley style. Flinty church called St Mary's.

Eating & Drinking

THE SWAN - Tel: 01491 878800. Highly regarded riverside hotel open to non-residents. Beautiful waterside gardens with an Oxford College barge permanently moored alongside. Al fresco meals in summer. RG8 9HR

South Stoke Map 27

Idyllic village isolated from the outside world by the river and the railway. The 13th century church notable for its glass. Other buildings use tile, thatch, flint and weatherboarding to much effect. Suitable moorings by the old ferry staithe.

Eating & Drinking

PERCH & PIKE - village centre. Tel: 01491 872415. Picture perfect inn offering food and accommodation. Lunch from noon, dinner (ex Sun) from 6pm. RG8 0JS

Moulsford Map 27

A corruption of 'Mules Ford'. The church is the work of George Gilbert Scott and lies hidden between the road and the riverbank. The inn gets its name from tools used in wood cutting; a 'beetle' being a heavy type of mallet. As well as being associated with H.G. Wells, another literary guest was G. B. Shaw.

Eating & Drinking

BEETLE & WEDGE BOATHOUSE - Ferry Lane. Tel: 01491 651381. Charming riverside eatery also offering accommodation. OX10 9JF

Cholsey Map 27

The Great War poet, Edward Thomas, crossed the Thames by ferry from Little Stoke to Cholsey and walked up the Papist Way while researching on foot his book *The Icknield Way*. In the bar of the Morning Star he eavesdropped as a drayman and a butcher's boy agreed that motor-cars were ruining the roads. What prescience, for this was 1912! Agatha Christie (under her married name of Mallowan) is buried in the isolated churchyard beyond the railway.

Connections

TRAINS - Great Western Railway services to/from London, Reading and Didcot. Tel: 0345 748 4950.

FORMING the boundary between Berkshire and Oxfordshire, the river makes attractive progress through a gracious landscape full of historical and natural interest. In the churchyard at Lower Basildon, Jethro Tull - previously encountered at Crowmarsh Gifford on Map 26 - is buried. Beale Park wildlife centre is home to many rare breeds and endangered species and has hosted the National Waterways Festival on two or three occasions.

Briefly, the Thames Path detours away from the riverbank, though any disappointment incurred is amply compensated for by being reunited with the river at an elevated vantage point amidst the beech and yew tree and chalk cliff setting of Hartslock Wood, the name of which recalls the existence of a former lock in the neighbourhood. Note that the path, chalky underfoot, becomes steep in places.

It does not come as any great surprise to learn that Kenneth Grahame, who wrote the incomparable children's classic, *The Wind in the Willows*, spent a good deal of his life in Pangbourne and was inspired in telling the story to his young son by the river scenery of his own boyhood. You too will fall for the beauty of these reaches of the Thames and, like Mole, be 'intoxicated with the sparkle, the ripple, the scents and the sounds and the sunlight'.

Whitchurch Toll Bridge, made of iron and built in 1902, was rebuilt in 2014, and now looks as good as new. Sensibilities alter with time, for Eric de Mare, the photographer, architectural writer and close friend of L. T. C. Rolt proclaimed the bridge 'no beauty' in his book *Time on the Thames* published in 1952. Over sixty years later its whitewashed span gleams appealingly below the lock, and by modern standards looks anything but ugly, and it is the hard-hearted motorist who begrudges his forty pence to cross so characterful a structure in such a gorgeous setting. Incidentally, the only other toll bridge on the Thames is at Swinford, some half dozen miles upstream of Oxford. The tiny River Pang enters the Thames shyly, having risen on the Berkshire Downs south of Didcot. On the reach down to Mapledurham, pupils from the Oratory School - founded in 1859 by Cardinal Newman - are put through their rowing paces.

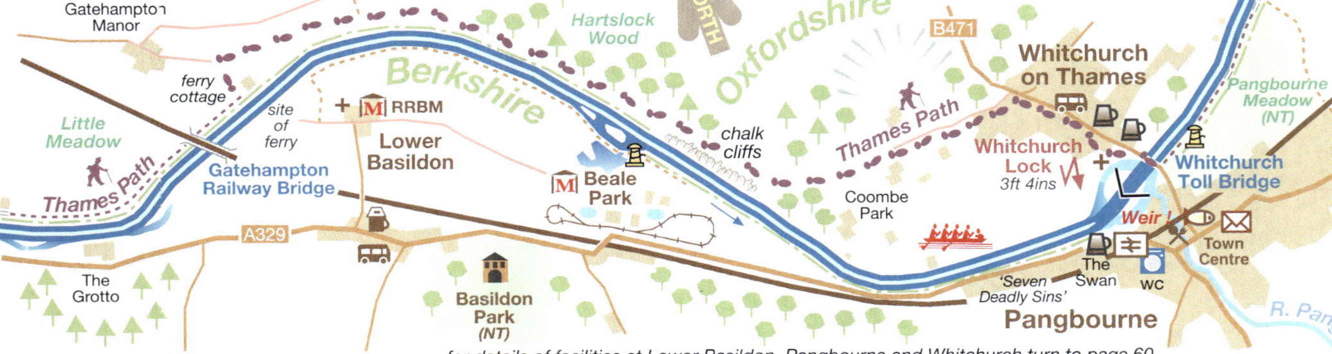

for details of facilities at Lower Basildon, Pangbourne and Whitchurch turn to page 60

Lower Basildon
Map 28

The delightful flint and brick church of St Bartholomew's is cared for by the estimable Churches Conservation Trust. In the churchyard two teenage brothers who drowned here in 1886, are poignantly remembered by a sculpture above their grave.

Things to Do
BEALE PARK - lovely wildlife sanctuary with moorings for visitors by boat. Miniature railway, adventure park, refreshments; deer, owls, goats, flamingos and lemurs. Tel: 0118 976 7480. RG8 9NH

RACING & RIVER BOAT MUSEUM - Old Tithe Barn, Lower Basildon. Charming collection of small river craft: dinghies, rowing boats, canoes et al. Open Wed-Sun 10am-5pm. RG8 9NH

BASILDON PARK - Tel: 01491 672382. 18th century Palladian mansion designed by John Carr (of York) for a man who made a fortune in India. National Trust. As seen on *Downton Abbey*! RG8 9NR

Pangbourne
Map 28

A row of elegant late Victorian houses which line the riverbank to the west of Pangbourne are known as the 'Seven Deadly Sins'. Lady Cunard, the socialite, was once a resident here, and these houses set the rather racy tone for a likeable little town marred only by a surfeit of road traffic. Public moorings are to be found on the Berkshire bank downstream from Whitchurch Toll Bridge. To reach the centre on foot you must negotiate a constricted tunnel under the four track railway. Kenneth Grahame lived at Church Cottage and when he died the church was decorated with fresh willows in honour of his famous book.

Eating & Drinking
DULCE DOMUM - The Square. Tel: 0118 984 2237. Restaurant and bar within George Hotel. RG8 7AJ

LINA TANDOORI - Whitchurch Road. Tel: 0118 984 5577. Indian restaurant. RG8 7BP

NINO'S - Reading Road. Tel: 0118 984 1333. Italian restaurant. RG8 7LR

THE SWAN - riverbank, moorings for customers. Tel: 0118 984 4494. Famous old Thameside inn fondly remembered as the spot where the Three Men and Montmorency shamefacedly abandoned their boat and caught the train back to Paddington and the Alhambra. Bar/restaurant meals. RG8 7DU
Plus wide choice of take-aways and coffee shops etc.

Shopping
A good collection of shops make Pangbourne a useful base. There's a Co-op convenience store (7am-10pm daily), and a branch of W. H. Smith. But it is the independents (as always) who catch the eye: Greens the butchers, and Cheese etc. Launderette near the station. Post Office in Collins hardware store.

Connections
TRAINS - frequent Great Western Railway services along the river corridor. Tel: 0345 748 4950.
TAXIS - Pangbourne Taxis. Tel: 01491 671979.

Whitchurch
Map 28

Peaceful and shopless, the picturesque houses of Whitchurch-on-Thames cling to a steep hill on the Oxfordshire bank of the Thames.

Eating & Drinking
THE FERRYBOAT - High Street. Tel: 0118 984 2161. Well appointed country pub and restaurant with nice courtyard garden for warm weather; closed Mondays. RG8 7DB

Lower Basildon

ESPITE the proximity of the main line railway and the strung out suburbs of Tilehurst (once linked umbilically by trolley-bus to Reading) the Thames retains its integrity, unimpeachably lovely however we care to compromise it. Reading is rapidly shaken off when travelling upstream, in the opposite direction it delays showing its urban hand until the last possible moment, and a plethora of handsome dwellings and boat houses (occasionally combined to sublime effect) line the well-heeled Caversham bank.

The demise of ferries at Mapledurham and Tilehurst forces walkers on the Thames Path into a diversion through the suburban environs of Purley, twenty minutes spent anxiously peering for signposts, dodging supermarket delivery vans and wondering if pampas grass - against all received scientific wisdom - really is indigenous to the Thames valley. Rolling hills and woods characterise the view to the north, the Chiltern escarpment. The environs of Mapledurham Lock - the first on the Thames to be mechanised in 1956 - are outstandingly scenic and a lockside tearoom (with plants for sale) adds to its popularity.

Mapledurham House is of 16th century origin and is widely considered one of England's finest Tudor buildings. It was home to the Catholic Blounts, a secret tunnel leads to the adjoining church. Royalists used secret rooms and passages within the house during the Civil War. John Galsworthy wrote the final chapters of his *Forsyte Saga* whilst staying in the house and E. H. Shepard who illustrated *The Wind in the Willows*, is said to have been inspired by the setting. The adjoining watermill (which featured on the cover of the eponymous album by Black Sabbath and also - in a *faux* Norfolk setting - in the film *The Eagle Has Landed*) has been restored and is open to the public on summer weekends. Hardwick House is even older than Mapledurham. Charles I graced it with his presence, albeit under close arrest!

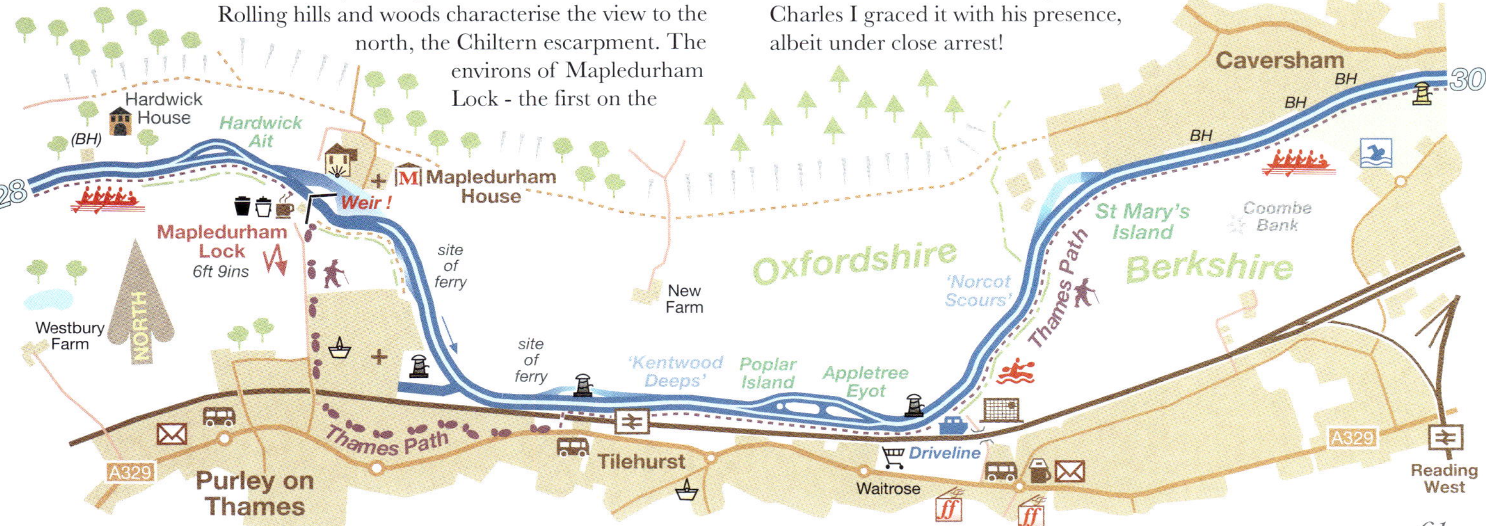

30 RIVER THAMES Reading 2mls/11k/1hr*

IF there's a seedy side to Reading, the traveller on, or beside the Thames is largely spared it. For once one does not necessarily concur with Jerome K. Jerome's opinion that the river at Reading is 'dismal and dirty', nor Roger Pilkington's view that it is 'down-at-heel and dreary'. However intrusive the architectural horizon might threaten to be, the meadowlands let the river off lightly, keeping urbanisation in its rightfully subliminal place.

Three bridges span the river as it skims the northern edge of the town. The present Caversham Bridge dates from 1926. In 1643 an earlier manifestation of the bridge was the scene of a battle between the Earl of Essex and Charles I during the Civil War. Downstream, Fry's Island plays host to a hire base and a bowling club whose 'Bohemian' members make use of a private ferry to gain access to their neatly mown greens. Playing bowls on an island sounds like the perfect escape; are they allowed eight discs as well? Christchurch foot and cycle bridge dates from 2015. Reading Bridge is three years the senior of Caversham. When constructed it was one of the longest concrete spans then in existence. To prove that it was up to the job, a convoy of steam road-rollers was driven onto it to confirm its load-bearing qualities. Sadly, that scene was not re-enacted after the structure's strengthening in 2015.

Caversham Lock lies in a bosky setting surrounded by parkland, and as such transcends its setting on the edge of a large town, feeling no more urban than Mapledurham upstream or Sonning down. Thames Lido re-opened in 2017. It first opened in 1902 as a Ladies Swimming

Bath but fell into disuse in the 1970s. Originally it drew its water from the Thames, but was converted to mains water supply in the 1950s. There were no windows, so as to preserve the privacy of Edwardian ladies.

Sundry islets mask backwaters and private moorings as the river glides down to Kennet Mouth. Visitor moorings are provided along the south bank alongside a 24 hour Tesco Extra supermarket occupying land once given over to a considerable amount of railway lines. From these long gone sidings a triangle of lines led into Huntley & Palmers biscuit factory, which Nick Deacon described in some detail in the industrial archaeological journal *Archive* - issue 108.

Overlooked by a gasholder ('the largest and strongest smelling' that Pilkington had ever seen) Kennet Mouth forms a misleadingly inauspicious beginning to the Kennet & Avon. The Thames Path is carried across the Kennet by an appendix to the main line railway bridge. The river leaves Reading behind along a straight known as Dreadnought Reach, a name derived from a former pub at Kennet Mouth. The building still remains, offering a faded signwritten clue to its local Simonds Brewery parentage. The extensive Thames & Kennet Marina occupies former gravel extraction workings. Port Fonty is home to the Thames Traditional Boat Society, formed in 1980 to preserve and conserve traditional unpowered craft associated with the river such as skiffs and punts. Also transformed from former gravel workings, the Redgrave-Pinsent Rowing Lake was opened by its eponymous Olympians in 2006. The Thames proceeds towards Sonning past watermeadows bordered by a sizeable business park.

SHAKING off Reading's business parks, whilst skirting former gravel workings reinvented as rowing courses, the river runs down to Sonning (pronounced 'Sunning'), 'the most fairy-like little nook on the whole river' according to Jerome K. Jerome. One might argue with his first choice, whilst broadly agreeing with his sentiments; for, a century or so on, Sonning retains its fairy-tale atmosphere which one writer has likened to a Hollywood ideal of England. The brick-built lock house dates from the First World War. On the towpath side an iron gate decorated with oars commemorates a master from the adjoining Blue Coat School drowned in the vicinity on 26th January 1953.

Sonning Mill ceased grinding out a living in 1969, by which time it was the last on the Thames deriving power from its water-wheels. In its heyday it had operated a fleet of barges to bring wheat up from the Port of London and to convey milled flour to Huntley & Palmers biscuit factory at Reading. Happily, the mill enjoys a new lease of life as a restaurant and theatre. The picturesque bridge - of whose eleven arches solely the centre is navigable - dates from the 17th century, and on this strollers on the Thames Path must cross, exchanging Berks for Oxon or vice versa. Downstream the river, lined by willows and reeds, threads low-lying pastures. The reach between Sonning and Shiplake

feels unconvincingly remote, and briefly you are reminded of the Upper Thames between Oxford and Lechlade, but airliners, stacked up on the approach to Heathrow, quickly belie this enjoyable though false sense of seclusion.

Three islets precede Shiplake which sits perched on a chalky outcrop above the boathouses of Shiplake College whose pupils wear rather elegant, predominantly red blazers with blue and yellow stripes which would not look out of place were they to be provided by the wardrobe department in a filmed dramatization of *Three Men In A Boat* : fortunate young people to be educated in so timeless an atmosphere.

Shiplake Lock is an idyllic spot, at its tail the River Loddon enters the Thames, some thirty miles from its chalk spring fed source near Basingstoke. A bridge carries the branch line railway which links the main line at Twyford with Henley, but, unlike the railway bridge downstream at Bourne End (Map 41), there is no provision here for pedestrians, other than by taking the train between Wargrave and Shiplake.

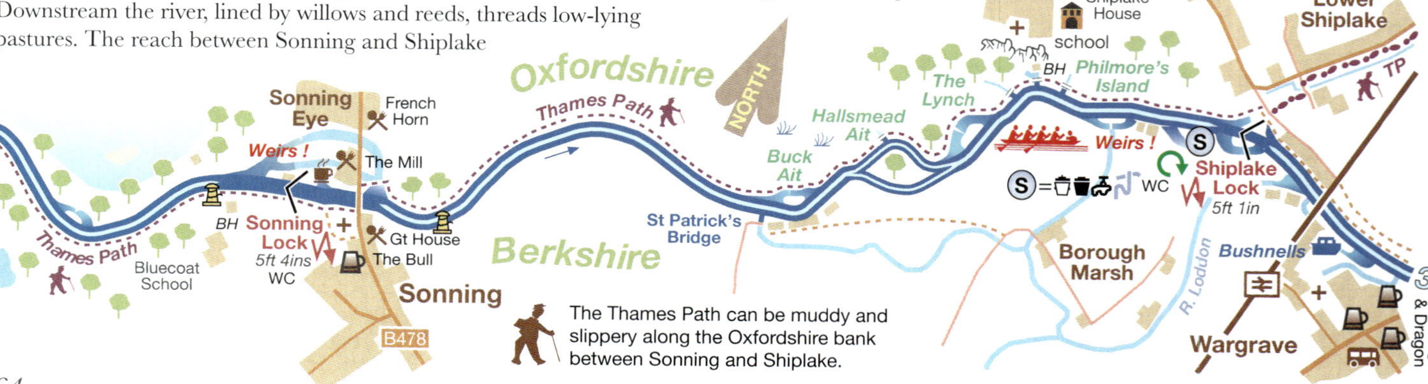

Sonning
Map 31

'Tinged with an Edwardian holiday, or musical-comedy, gaiety' wrote Betjeman & Piper in 1949 and you can still see where they were coming from; money doesn't talk here so much as discreetly whisper. The Bishops of Salisbury had a palace near the imposing church, but perhaps the village's best building is Lutyens' Deanery Garden, built for the founder of *Country Life*. South of the Great West Road, Sonning Cutting is a two miles long, sixty foot deep gash engineered by Brunel (along with 1,220 navvies and 196 horses) in 1840 to effect the Great Western Railway's progress from London to Reading. Now mellowed by tree growth but once beloved of railway photographers. A blue plaque outside the Red House commemorates the fact that the playwright Terence Rattigan lived here 1945-7. Current village residents include a certain couple called Clooney.

Eating & Drinking

THE BULL - High Street. Tel: 0118 969 3901 Historic half-timbered inn recommended by Jerome K. Jerome in 1889, and time has not withered his opinion. Now owned by Fuller's, the Chiswick brewers who provide bar food, restaurant meals and accommodation to a high but not hugely expensive standard. RG4 6UP
GREAT HOUSE HOTEL - Thames Street (riverside). Tel: 0118 969 2277. Coppa Club restaurant with waterside garden. Customer moorings. RG4 6UT
FRENCH HORN HOTEL - Sonning Eye. Tel: 0118 969 2204. Luxury hotel and gourmet restaurant with lawns sloping down to the backwater. RG4 6TN
THE MILL AT SONNING - Sonning Eye. Tel: 0118 969 8000 Former 18th century flour mill (which retains a working water wheel) now imaginatively used as a Dinner Theatre where your meal is followed by a theatrical or musical performance - a lovely way to while away an afternoon or evening. Booking recommended. RG4 6TY
Seasonal tea room lockside.

Wargrave
Map 31

Wargrave church was rebuilt in 1916 after suffering an arson attack by the Suffragettes. In the churchyard there is a mausoleum by Lutyens. On High Street look out for the art-nouveau styling of Woodclyffe Hall.

Eating & Drinking

ST GEORGE & DRAGON - riverside. Tel: 0118 940 4474. Smartly refurbished inn offering customer moorings (not overnight). RG10 8HY
Cafe and two more pubs in the village.

Connections

TRAINS - halt on the Great Western Railway's 'Regatta Line' (see Henley). Tel: 0345 748 4950.
BUSES - Arriva service 850 operates hourly Mon-Sat to/from High Wycombe, Marlow, Henley and Reading. Tel: 0871 200 2233.

Sonning Bridge

32 RIVER THAMES Shiplake & Henley 4½ mls/11k/1hr

THE absence of two ferries forces the Thames Path in a diversion away from the riverbank and through Lower Shiplake instead, bringing advantages and disadvantages to boaters and walkers in almost equal measure: the former miss the roadside entrances to some fine properties (one of which boasts a magnificent miniature railway complete with a scaled down version of a Germanic looking station building) the latter these selfsame properties' sublime river frontages. Reed-lined and shallow, Hennerton Backwater can only realistically be navigated by small unpowered craft.

Between Ferry Eyot and Marsh Lock (and, indeed, all the way down to Henley) the river banks boast some remarkably handsome houses, many of which incorporate boathouses from which you can imagine teak launches emerging with elaborately costumed boating parties in the river's Victorian and Edwardian heyday. The Berkshire bank rises in a bluff of chalky cliff faces, and the A321 spans a lane running down to the waterside on a rough-hewn bridge erected in the 18th century

with stones garnered from the ruins of Reading Abbey. Intriguingly, this curious structure was built by the Rev. Humphrey Gainsborough, brother of the famous painter.

Elongated timber footbridges carry pedestrians over the backwaters and former millstreams either side of Marsh Lock. Once there were mills on either bank; one engaged in grinding flour the other a brass foundry. Humphrey Gainsborough is said to have been instrumental in construction of the first pound lock here in 1773.

Henley presents a welcoming face to river travellers. Counter-intuitively, the Thames, as it passes beneath Henley's much photographed bridge, is flowing north. There are excellent mooring facilities (albeit with a fee payable overnight) either side of the handsome five arch bridge which dates from 1787.

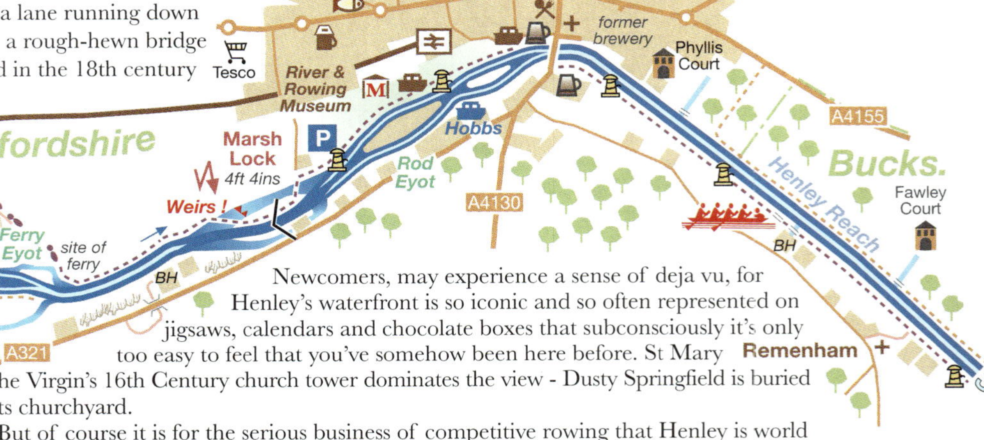

Newcomers, may experience a sense of deja vu, for Henley's waterfront is so iconic and so often represented on jigsaws, calendars and chocolate boxes that subconsciously it's only too easy to feel that you've somehow been here before. St Mary the Virgin's 16th Century church tower dominates the view - Dusty Springfield is buried in its churchyard.

But of course it is for the serious business of competitive rowing that Henley is world famous. The Regatta (held between the end of June and the beginning of July) dates back to

1839 and was conferred 'Royal' status in 1851. The Regatta course stretches from Temple Island to a point four hundred yards downstream of Henley Bridge. When it is in full flow, passing boaters are ushered through the 1 mile and 550 yards long course as expeditiously as possible, in full gaze of the well-dressed (and often well-oiled) throng: twelve thousand pints of Pimms; four and a half thousand bottles of champagne; and a ton of strawberries being consumed with gusto per annum. To those more versed in the utilitarian world of the canals, it is an experience not easily lived down.

The Regatta headquarters, opened by the Queen in 1986, stand alongside the town bridge on the Berkshire bank, cheek by jowl with the elaborate Edwardian premises of the Leander Rowing Club. Across the water two of Henley's most historic hostelries, The Angel and The Red Lion, return their gaze with interest. Downstream on the Oxfordshire bank the tower and maltings of Brakspear's former brewery loom over the rooftops of riverside houses and then there are some ebullient Edwardian properties boasting balconies and boat houses which must have some racy stories to relate could mere bricks and mortar but talk.

The Thames Path elopes with the Berkshire bank downstream of Henley Bridge. Henley Reach is overlooked by Phyllis Court, a prestigious gentlemen's club and Fawley Court, the work of Sir Christopher Wren. Of more import to males of a certain age is the exciting truth that Jenny Agutter was married in Remenham church. Caleb Gould, Hambleden's lock-keeper for almost sixty years, was buried in the churchyard in 1836.

Lower Shiplake — Map 32

No easy access for boaters, but a useful stop on the Thames Path with pub, post office stores, butcher and railway station.

Henley on Thames — Map 32

Synonymous with Pimms and brightly-striped blazers, outside the rush of Regatta week, Henley regresses, morphing back into its traditional role of a country market town, albeit a well-heeled example of the breed as exemplified by a profusion of eating places and upmarket emporiums. Mill Meadows with its grassy swards and ice cream parlours instils a seaside feel to the proceedings, and it would be churlish to begrudge parting with a 'tenner' to moor here overnight. Mill Meadows, and the adjoining Marsh Meadows are maintained as wetland habitats.

Eating & Drinking

THE ANGEL ON THE BRIDGE - Thames Side. Tel: 01491 410678. Iconic pub offering bar and restaurant food with terrace overlooking the bridge. RG9 1BH
BISTRO AT THE BOATHOUSE - Station Road. Tel: 01491 577937. Restaurant ex Mon & Tue. RG9 1AZ
HOTEL DU VIN - New Street. Tel: 01491 877579. Hotel with bistro open to non-residents in original Brakspear brewery premises. RG9 2BP
THE LITTLE ANGEL - Remenham Lane. Tel: 01491 411008. Smart refurbished pub across the river. RG9 2LS
SHELLFISH COW - Reading Road. Tel: 01491 578130. Independent restaurant/bar. RG9 1AB
SPICE MERCHANT - Thameside. Tel: 01491 636118. Contemporary Indian overlooking the river. RG9 2LJ
THREE TUNS - Market Place. Tel: 01491 410138. Congenial Brakspear gastropub. RG9 2AA
VILLA MARINA - Thameside. Tel: 01491 575262. Italian restaurant. RG9 1BH.

Shopping

A charming town to do your shopping in - Thursday is market day. There are two good antiquarian booksellers - Jonkers on Hart Street, and Way's on Friday Street - plus one of those increasingly rare but commendable independent booksellers called The Bell Bookshop located eponymously on Bell Street, where you'll also find Waitrose. In the Market Place, Gabriel Machin is an outstanding butcher's shop. Post Office on Reading Road. From the moorings which run along the west bank from the town centre to Marsh Lock, there is easy access on Mill Lane past the local football ground and over the railway to a large Tesco.

Things to Do

TOURIST INFORMATION - Town Hall. Tel: 01491 578034. RG9 2AQ
RIVER & ROWING MUSEUM - Mill Meadows. Tel: 01491 415600. Exceptionally well designed and interesting museum devoted to the River Thames, rowing, Henley itself and the *Wind in the Willows*. Excellent audio-visual aids, shop and cafe. RG9 1BF

Connections

TRAINS - approximately hourly Great Western Railway shuttle (branded the 'Regatta line') to/from Twyford with local connections thence to Reading or Paddington. Tel: 0345 748 4950.
BUSES - Arriva services 800/850 trundle along the scenic Thames Valley between Reading and High Wycombe via Henley and Marlow and many of the villages between. Thames Travel 'River Rapids' service X38 links Henley with Wallingford. Tel: 0871 200 2233.

PUTTING Henley's famous rowing course behind it, the Thames progresses downstream past a sequence of fascinating houses, all with a history to tell. Temple Island originally belonged to the owners of Fawley Court. The 'temple' itself was designed as a fishing lodge in 1771 by James Wyatt. The river curves round to Hambleden Lock past the white stucco spread of Greenlands, now a business school, but originally the home of William Henry Smith, and amusingly described by the narrator of *Three Men In A Boat* as 'the residence of my newsagent', for the man in question was, of course, the founder of the retail chain W. H. Smith.

The river is wide hereabouts and backed by stately wooded hills to the north. Hambleden Lock is overlooked by a picturesque weatherboarded mill, long since converted from the real business of corn milling into expensive accommodation. A mile north of Mill End lies the quintessentially English village of Hambleden, and its outlandishly euphonious neighbours Fingest, Frieth and Skirmett.

The demise of Aston Ferry again forces the Thames Path away from the riverbank, but by way of consolation the detour offers walkers the opportunity of refreshment at the Flower Pot Hotel, an unspoilt inn still charmingly advertising that it provides 'good accommodation for fishing and boating parties'. Walkers are also treated to a close-up view of Culham Court and its impressive topiary. George III was a guest here once and warm rolls wrapped in hot flannel by his favourite baker in London were rushed down to the pampered king by horse relay.

Alarm spread rapidly through these riparian meadows in 1897 when the Great Western Railway proposed linking its termini at Henley and Marlow with a new double-track line. Oarsmen and landowners united in outrage at the railway company's planned disfigurement of *their* river. The line would have had to have run along the Berkshire bank to avoid high ground and the erection of two substantial new bridges would have been required to cross the Thames. Palliative assurances that these bridges were to be of 'ornamental trellis character' did nothing to appease the protesters.

Medmenham Abbey bore witness to the debauched orgies of the

infamous Hellfire Club in the middle of the 18th century, but the history of the site goes back much further to the establishment of a Cistercian foundation whose monks were allegedly much better behaved. Danesfield House (built for a man who made his fortune in soap) looks disdainfully down across the river to a static caravan park; there could hardly be a greater contrast in the provision of accommodation for the same species. Danesfield (aka RAF Medmenham) was requisitioned by the Air Ministry during World War II and became a hush-hush centre for the interpretation of aerial photographs of enemy territory; culminating in its involvement in Operation Crossbow to destroy rocket sites in Northern France. The house is now a luxury hotel and spa.

An archipelago of wooded islands add mystery and atmosphere to the backwaters of Hurley Lock. Glimpsed amidst the trees, Harleyford Manor is one of several grand Thames-side houses said to have been the inspiration for Toad Hall. Freebodys are a famous Thames boatyard dedicated to the preservation of traditional craft. And whilst their inimitable owner, Peter Freebody, died in 2010, the company remain committed to his widely admired tenets.

Medmenham
Map 33

Now that the Hellfire orgies have abated, this is a peaceful spot and it appears possible to moor upstream of the conspicuous monument which commemorates a successful legal action brought in 1899 by Viscount Devonport to confirm the ferry's public, as opposed to private, status; a hollow victory, for the boat ceased plying between the wars. Stroll up to the Dog & Badger and you'll pass a garden containing two large Boer War cannons.

Eating & Drinking
YE OLDE DOG & BADGER - Ferry Lane (on A4155 approximately half a mile from the river. Tel: 01491 579944. Refurbished bar and restaurant dating from the 14th century. Accommodation. SL7 2HE

Connections
BUSES - services 800/850 and X80 connect with Henley and Marlow. Tel: 0871 200 2233.

Aston
Map 33

Eating & Drinking
THE FLOWER POT - Tel: 01491 574721. Idyllic Brakspear pub in the image of 'The Potwell Inn'. Decidedly free range poultry roam the beer garden. Rough moorings by the site of the ferry or walk back from above Hambleden Lock. RG9 3DG

Hurley
Map 33

Trance-like village which once boasted a Benedictine Priory, but now plays host to a static caravan park. One of Berkshire's most extensive parishes, it extends southwards to an area formerly quarried for chalk, the exhausted workings of which were used to conceal underground munitions works during the Second World War. Chillingly, at the time of the Cold War these were earmarked for use as a Regional Seat of Government in the event of nuclear conflict.

Eating & Drinking
YE OLDE BELL - village centre. Tel: 01628 825881. Half-timbered, flower bedecked hotel with gorgeous garden. SL6 5LX
RISING SUN - village centre. Tel: 01628 825733. Demure, family-run neighbour! SL6 5LT
Seasonal tea room lockside.

Shopping
Community run village store which has featured in *Midsomer Murders* ... just step over the corpses.

Connections
BUSES - Courtney Coaches service 239 provides a sparse but potentially useful link Mon, Wed, Fri & Sat with Henley and Maidenhead. Tel: 0871 200 2233.

THE pound between Hurley and Temple locks is the second shortest on the Thames. Temple Footbridge was erected in 1989 to replace a ferry abandoned over forty years earlier. Bland housing occupies the site of a former foundry which once received copper by boat from South Wales via the Thames & Severn Canal. A rock located beside the towpath commemorates Giles Every, a local rowing enthusiast who was killed in a motoring accident in 1984.

Bisham Abbey is now an internationally acclaimed centre for sports development, all a far cry from the days when it was presented to Anne of Cleves by Henry VIII by way of consolation for his decision to divorce her: Queen Elizabeth I is said to have spent some of her childhood here. Bisham's picturesque parish church also adorns the Berkshire bank, being feted for its Hoby chapel and monuments.

Marlow lies roughly half way between Oxford and London. The suspension bridge which spans the river at Marlow dates from 1832 and is the work of an engineer called William Tierney Clark. He later went on to design a larger suspension bridge linking Buda on one bank of the Danube with Pest on the other.

In Eric de Mare's opinion the structure is a good example of 'that period when engineering and architecture enjoyed a brief but happy marriage' and 'forms an excellent foil to the spire' of All Saints Church, an exact contemporary. Perhaps the best view of these mutually inclusive but unlikely bedfellows is upstream from Marlow Lock, employing the natural perspective of the curving weir to draw the eye towards both church and bridge. This is one of the Thames' most definitive scenes, and the sole disappointment lies in the niggling absence now of Marlow Mill which used to make flour from locally produced grain and paper from rags brought upstream from London by barge. In the Philistine Sixties, the millstream was dammed, the mill demolished, and apartments erected in a not entirely unsuccessful parody of their predecessor.

Downstream from Marlow Lock the river passes beneath the town's noisy by-pass but quickly finds balm as it skirts the wooded slopes of Quarry Wood, said to have been the inspiration for Kenneth Grahame's Wild Wood. Neighbouring Winter Hill is terraced by spectacular houses whose views, one imagines, can only be classified sublime. On the Buckinghamshire side rugby pitches are separated

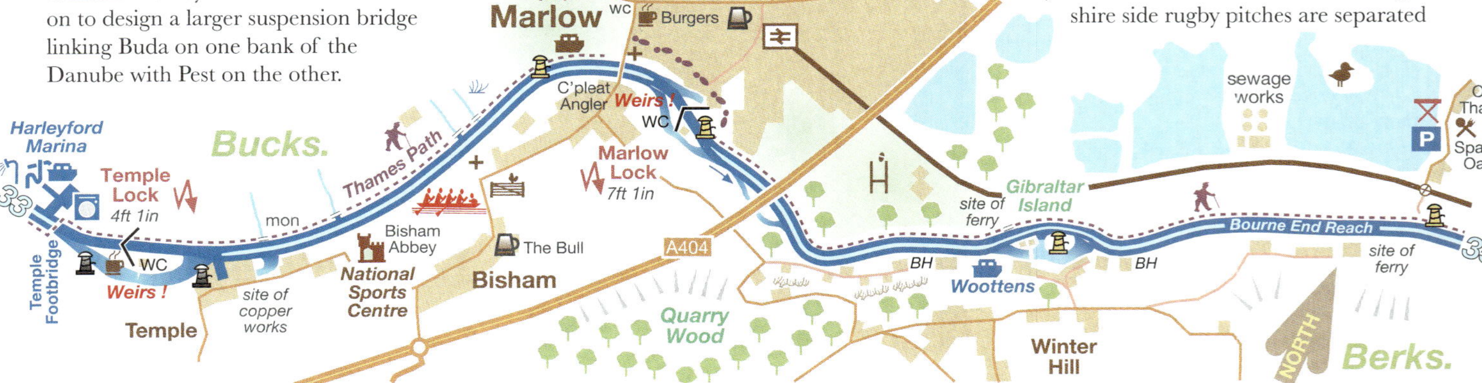

from the water's edge by a narrow belt of woodland with benches and picnic tables.

Marlow's branch line railway shadows the river's progress. Once this was the lair of the 'Marlow Donkey', a diminutive push & pull train which spent its life plying to and from Bourne End, where connections were made with the trains which formerly linked High Wycombe with Maidenhead. Construction of the independent Great (sic) Marlow Railway commenced in 1872. Intriguingly, the engineer was locally-born Edwin Clark who, three years later, designed the Anderton boat lift linking the Trent & Mersey Canal to the Weaver Navigation. Small (waterways) world! Dabbling in law and pedagogy, and in danger of being labelled a dilettante, Clark found his metier in engineering, having been introduced to Robert Stephenson, who was impressed enough to engage him in construction of the Britannia Bridge across the Menai Strait. To an engineer of Clark's eminence, building a short branch line across the flat meadow-lands of the Thames Valley must have seemed like child's play, but as a Marlow man he urged his townsfolk to stop dithering and build a railway to the outside world, considering it 'of no small importance to get the name of our town inserted in Bradshaw'! Up until the inevitable Beechingesque rationalisations of the 1960s, the Donkey's shuttling was supplemented by lengthy excursion trains from far afield, often run in conjunction with the sailings of Salters steamers.

There are visitor moorings at the site of Spade Oak Ferry, which sadly ceased plying in 1956. Beyond the level crossing, a by-road leads past the eponymous pub to a house called Old Thatch where Enid Blyton wrote many of her stories for children.

Marlow   Map 34

The configuration of park, church and river bridge smacks of Henley, but Marlow is far more demure. Like Henley, however - and, for that matter Abingdon as well - Marlow is a town whose brewery, once a major employer, has closed down; in this case it was Wethered's who fell prey to Whitbread and closed in 1988. You cannot, though, fail to progess far up the High Street without encountering the brewery's husk, an ache for those mindful of regionality, however amenably converted into housing and offices. Throughout the town there are some fine buildings, particularly from the Georgian era, and a very real feeling of well-being pervades the streets. A series of statues and plaques recall some of Marlow's famous sons and daughters: an impresario who foundered with the *Lusitania* in 1915; Edward John Gregory, the painter of Boulter's Lock (Map 35); T. S. Eliot; Edwin Clark (see above); Thomas Love Peacock the novelist and his friends the Shelleys, of whom Mary is said to have written *Frankenstein* here.

Eating & Drinking

BURGERS - The Causeway. Tel: 01628 483389. Swiss owned tearoom, craft baker and chocolatier. Breakfasts, omelettes and Swiss Rarebit! SL7 1NF
COMPLEAT ANGLER - Marlow Bridge. Tel: 01628 484444. Inspired by Izaak Walton, this long established hotel is part of the Macdonald group with Riverside Restaurant, Sindhu Indian and Walton Bar. SL7 1RG
COTE - West Street. Tel: 01628 481459. Reliable French chain from 8am (9am weekends).SL7 2LS
GIGGLING SQUID - West Street. Tel: 01628 483047. Increasingly popular Thai chain. SL7 2NB
THE MARLOW DONKEY - Station Road. Tel: 01628 482022. Greene King pub recalling the name of the local push & pull train. SL7 1NW
VANILLA POD - West Street. Tel: 01628 898101. *Good Food Guide* and Michelin listed dining in building where T. S. Eliot once lived. SL7 2LS
ZIZZI'S - High Street. Tel: 01628 890200. Contemporary Italian chain housed in part of old brewery. SL7 1AQ

Shopping

It is probably no longer feasible to effect a triumphant exit from provisioning here in the manner of Jerome K. Jerome, George, Harris and Montmorency along with a cortege of shop boys, but nowadays Marlow lacks nothing in the Thames Valley's recurring theme of sophisticated shopping. There is a Sainsbury's and Marks & Spencer Food Hall within easy bag-carrying distance of the river. Small retail market on Wednesdays and Saturdays; Farmers' Market on Sundays. Marlow Bookshop on Spittal Street.

Things to Do

MARLOW MUSEUM - Pound Lane. Tel: 01628 485474. Well displayed local history in riverside park. SL7 2AE

Connections

BUSES - Arriva services 800/850, together with Carousel X80, provide frequent links for Marlow with High Wycombe to the north-east and Reading via Henley to the south-west. Tel: 0871 200 2233.
TRAINS - Great Western Railway links with Bourne End, Cookham and Maidenhead. Tel: 0345 748 4950.

ART, politics and wealth are the sub-texts of this section of the Thames, and for many these reaches mark the river's apotheosis. The delightful premises of the Upper Thames Sailing Club (founded in 1884) set the tone for Bourne End, a jaunty riverside village. The preserved steamer *Alaska* was built in Bourne End in 1883 and, three years later, acquired by Salters who put it to work on the Oxford to Kingston service. A footnote in Salters timetable informed passengers that they had to arrange to be ferried out to passing steamers in the absence of a suitable jetty.

The Thames Path crosses sides by way of a footbridge cantilevered out from the railway bridge in recent years to remedy a conspicuous absence of ferries, of which no fewer than four have perished. When opened in 1854, the railway was laid to Brunel's 'broad gauge' and the original bridge was of timber construction. A post beside the track reveals that Paddington is twenty-eight and a half miles away; by boat - via Brentford and Bulls Bridge - it's fifty-five!

Cock Marsh is a Site of Special Scientific Interest, a throwback landscape somehow inured from the pressures of Thames Valley expansionism. Backed by a furzy escarpment, the Berkshire bank contrasts markedly with the residental glamour of the Buckinghamshire side of the river.

Cookham Reach is another prone to dinghy manoeuvres, but it leads expansively down to Stanley Spencer's former abode, revelling in scenes which inspired one of the greatest, not to say idiosyncratic, of 20th century painters who was in the habit of wheeling his painting materials around the neighbourhood in a pram. Cookham Bridge is a Victorian structure of cast iron construction, made by a foundry as far away as Darlington! These days it is painted a pale and lacklustre blue, but in Spencer's painting *Swan Upping at Cookham* it appears more attractively in brown and green.

Three missing ferries force the Thames Path away from the riverbank in the vicinity of Cookham, and this is a great shame because the lock cut, dating from 1830, is especially lovely, even by the high standards of the Thames. Accessible on foot from Cookham village, it's a popular resort where refreshments are available from a lockside kiosk. The county boundary between Bucks and Berks follows Hedsor Water, the former main channel of the river. Once there was a busy wharf at Hedsor from which paper manufactured at a nearby mill

for details of facilities at Bourne End and Cookham turn to page 74

was conveyed downstream.

'You can't walk by the river at Cliveden Reach and not believe in God' was Stanley Spencer's firm belief, but the environs had an altogether different impact on John Profumo when he was a guest of Viscount Astor at Cliveden in July 1961; encountering not a deity but a naked nemesis in a swimming pool. Her name was Christine Keeler, and the rest, as they say, is pruriently-documented history. But this chance meeting hastened the demise of an hitherto imperious Conservative government and, along with the Lady Chatterley case and the Beatles' first LP, a purblind age of post-war innocence. Cliveden can trace its origins back to the 17th Century. In 1668 the Duke of Buckingham killed the Earl of Shrewsbury in a duel on the terrace. *Rule Britannia* was first performed here at a masque in 1740, under the baton of Thomas Arne, its composer. Three disastrous fires spelt an end to its earlier manifestations, and the present mansion, designed by Charles Barry for the Duke of Sutherland, dates from 1851. It belongs to the National Trust who sub-let it as an hotel. It enjoyed a heyday under the ownership of the wealthy Astor family and gained a dubious reputation in the mid 1930s when the 'Cliveden Set' of movers and shakers propagated appeasement with Nazi Germany. Look back on it from Bavin's Gulls (a group of slender wooded islets, as opposed to a particularly debilitating disease) to see it at its vainglorious best. A trio of Arts & Crafts style cottages overlook the riverbank, the furthest downstream being Spring Cottage, built for the Duchess of Sutherland in 1857 by George Devey for use as a summer house. This is where Christine Keeler was staying as a guest of Stephen Ward before the Profumo scandal broke. In earlier days the Duchess would entertain

Stanley Spencer's grave, Cookham

Queen Victoria to tea in the secluded garden. Nowadays it's available for exclusive holiday lets through the hotel. In the adjoining boat house a flotilla of vintage launches is maintained for the amusement of Cliveden guests. Turner's *Barge on the River, Sunset*, painted in 1805, illustrates bargemen mooring for the night on Cliveden Reach.

A footbridge carries the Thames Path over White Brook as the outer suburbs of Maidenhead begin to make their presence felt. Some extensive Edwardian properties line the river. In one of them, Islet Park House, the puppeteer, Gerry Anderson, made some of his early television programmes such as *Torchy the Battery Boy* and *Four Feather Falls*, before going on to greater things with *Thunderbirds*.

On the approach to Boulter's Lock, the Jubilee River leaves the main channel and commences its seven mile course, rejoining the Thames below Black Potts Bridge between Windsor and Datchet (Map 37). Opened in 2002 to alleviate the Thames' propensity to cause flooding in the vicinity of Maidenhead and Windsor, the man-made watercourse has not been without its critics, though trouble was taken to lend it a natural air, and it enjoys considerable leisure use, not least in that it is accompanied by National Cycle Route 61.

Boulter's Lock was made famous by E. J. Gregory's 1898 painting depicting it thronged with pleasure craft on a *fin de siecle* Sunday afternoon presided over by the redoutable lock-keeper W. H. Turner and his faithful hound Juggins. For those already familiar with Gregory's ebullient picture, reality is something of a let down, as the modern day lock setting is compromised by a suburban road and the gaudy canopies of an ice cream kiosk.

Bourne End
Map 35

Behind the riverbank's pretty facade, Edwardian villas give way to suburbia, and the jauntiness subsides.

Eating & Drinking

THE BOUNTY - Cock Marsh (riverside upstream of rail bridge on Berkshire bank). Tel: 01628 520056. Homely and welcoming *Good Beer Guide* listed pub self-billed as the People's Republic of Cockmarsh. Sixty metres of mooring decking for patrons. SL8 5RG

KEG - Wooburn Green. Tel: 01628 529369. Craft beers, ciders and gins. SL8 5QN

LAST VICEROY - The Parade. Tel: 01628 531383. Indian restaurant. SL8 5SS

SMILES - The Parade. Tel: 01628 521968. Eat in or take-away fish & chips. SL8 5SS

SPADE OAK - Coldmoorholme Lane (Map 34). Tel: 01628 520090. Pub/restaurant at the end of a quiet cul de sac and reached via a railway crossing from good moorings upstream of Bourne End. Rebellion beer from the Marlow Brewery. SL8 5PS
There are also Indian and Chinese restaurants.

Shopping

Suburban shopping featuring convenience stores, a pharmacy, butcher, grocery, newsagent/post office, off-licence, bakery, bike shop, Lloyds and NatWest banks.

Connections

BUSES - Arriva service 37 links High Wycombe (for trains to/from the midlands) Mon-Sat with Maidenhead via Cookham. Tel: 0871 200 2233.

TRAINS - Great Western Railway branchline services to/from Marlow and Maidenhead. Tel: 0345 748 4950.

Cookham
Map 35

Cookham dwells rather smugly on its riverbank and Stanley Spencer lies in its churchyard, doubtless ruminating on the unforgiving march of property values, and the misplacement of other more important values. Cookham Moor is a wide open landscape looked after by the National Trust.

Eating & Drinking

ANONG THAI - High Street. Tel: 01628 532027. Restaurant and take-away. SL6 9SJ

BEL & THE DRAGON - High Street. Tel: 01628 521263. Restaurant/rooms with smart interior and 'contemporary' garden for al fresco eating. SL6 9SQ

SPICE MERCHANT - High Street. Tel: 01628 522584. Indian restaurant. SL6 9SL

THE CROWN - High Street. Tel: 01628 520163. Half-timbered pub overlooking Cookham Moor which offers B&B. SL6 9SB

THE FERRY - Sutton Road. Tel: 01628 525123. Smart pub with waterside terrace and moorings. SL6 9SN

MALIK'S - High Street. Tel: 01628 520085. Tandoori. SL6 9SF

PEKING INN - High Street. Tel: 01628 520900. Chinese restaurant and take-away. SL6 9SL

TEA POT - High Street. Tel: 01628 529514. Charming tea room daily (ex Mon) 10am-5pm. SL6 9SJ

Shopping

You have to go to Cookham Rise for proper food shops. There you'll come across a well stocked convenience store by the station and then, perhaps a quarter of a mile beyond the level crossing, a post office, an outlet dealing in wood-burning stoves, a butcher and the splendid Deliciously French deli (Tel: 01628 819114). Pretty much all the other businesses in Cookham itself are devoted to ladies fashions and/or beauty parlours. While their womenfolk are so engaged, mere males can patronize a fine wine merchant and/or a nice little model railway shop.

Things to Do

SPENCER GALLERY - High Street. Tel: 01628 531092. Former Methodist Chapel converted as a shrine to this most parochial yet talented of 20th century English painters who was born at the house called Fernlea on High Street in 1891. Open daily April to October, Thur-Sun November to March. SL6 9SJ

CLIVEDEN - access for boaters via National Trust moorings on Cliveden Reach which are idyllic, if informal, and there is an overnight charge. Tel: 01628 605069. 'Camelot-on-Thames' is how Nancy Astor was wont to describe Cliveden, Charles Barry's ostentatiously Italianate mansion built for the Duke of Sutherland in 1851. The house itself, now a luxurious hotel - Tel: 01628 668561 (SL6 0JF) - is only partially open to the public under the auspices of the National Trust on a couple of afternoons per week, but the enchanting grounds more than make up for this, both in the formal gardens and the woodland walks. The former Ferry Cottage and its neighbour, New Cottage, are available for NT holiday lets.

Connections

BUSES - Arriva service 37 runs Mon-Sat to/from Bourne End and High Wycombe and Cookham Rise and Maidenhead. Tel: 0871 200 2233.

TRAINS - as Bourne End.

Taplow
Map 36

BOULTERS - Boulter's Lock, (Map 35) Maidenhead. Tel: 01628 621291. Brasserie and terrace bar. SL6 8PE

ROUX AT SKINDLES - Mill Lane. Tel: 01628 951100. Contemporary brasserie. SL6 0AA

THAI ORCHID - Ray Mead Road. Tel: 01628 777555. Riverside Thai restaurant. SL6 8NJ

Bray
Map 36

Idyllic waterside village formerly famous for its 17th century vicar and his weathercock attitude to politics and religion, but now renowned as a centre for fine-dining. Take your pick between Heston Blumenthal's Fat Duck (Tel: 01628 580333 - SL6 2AQ) or the Roux family's Waterside Inn (Tel: 01628 620691 - SL6 2AT).

FLOWING north to south, the Thames skims Maidenhead and finds itself spanned by three great trade routes: the old Great West (or Bath) Road, the Great Western Railway, and the M4 Motorway. The gracious lines of Maidenhead Bridge date from 1772. It is the work of Sir Robert Taylor, and if you mentally filter out the dross of its 21st Century surroundings, you can't help but picture stage coaches trundling over it, Bath bound in the age of Beau Brummell.

It is a generality that successive bridges lack the panache of their predecessors, and suffer by comparison. At Maidenhead, however, Brunel's railway bridge - Taylor's junior by sixty-seven years - wins all the plaudits, not least in its status as the flattest and widest brick arch in the world. As it was being built, lesser men than Brunel predicted its collapse with confidence. Some aural response to the ellipticity of the arches creates a spectacular echo which you may care to try out. *The Laughing Policeman* works particularly well.

Between Maidenhead and Bray the Berkshire bank of the river plays host to many sumptuous houses, though some illustrate a greater awareness of the value of wealth than good taste. Some of the older, more demure

properties hark back to the *fin de siecle* days of the 19th Century when it became something of a vogue for society mothers to summer their daughters here in the hope that they might attract the attention of officers from the nearby Brigade of Guards club.

Bray Lock leads to Dorney Reach. The M4 spans the river on a bridge dating from 1961 which makes no attempt to emulate the aestheticism of either of the bridges at Maidenhead. Monkey Island is home to a wedding cake confection of an hotel housed in a building built in 1738 by the Duke of Marlborough for use as a fishing lodge. Another notable house in the vicinity - now known as Long White Cloud (the Maori name for New Zealand) but formerly rather more prosaically as The Hut - belonged to Frank Shuster, a patron of the arts who numbered Elgar, Shaw, Sassoon and Arnold Bennett amongst his friends, and much of Elgar's Violin Concerto was composed here. In later years it was the childhood home of the racing driver Stirling Moss.

Cheek by jowl stand Down Place

and Oakley Court, two elaborate properties which have certainly 'seen life'. Down Place became Bray (Film) Studios in the 1950s and here the Hammer Film Production Co. made their celebrated low budget horror movies. Oakley Court was also used by the film industry at one time, but is now an hotel.

ETON and Windsor regard each other across the Thames with what appears to be mutual admiration, and certainly they have the knack of attracting large numbers of visitors, many of whom make it their business to take to the water in one way or another - you have been warned!

Upstream, the river negotiates Boveney Lock, above which a backwater leads from the rear of Bush Ait to Racecourse Marina and extensive private moorings. Boveney Chapel - dedicated to St Mary Magdalene - is cared for by the Friends of Friendless Churches. It dates from the Norman Conquest and largely gleaned its congregation from the ranks of river bargemen.

'Athens' was the sobriquet given to a quiet bathing place on the north bank of the river by generations of Etonians. A commemorative stone recalls one John Lionel Baker, killed in a flying accident in 1917. On the river-most side of the stone a notice lists Bathing Regulations, not least that boys who are undressed must conceal themselves - either in the water or behind screens - when 'boats containing ladies come in sight'. Boveney Ditch enters the river just upstream of this point and nowadays carries the county boundary, for Berkshire has 'upped sticks' and requisitioned Eton and Slough since the crass and uncalled for re-organisations of the mid-nineteen-seventies. Royal Windsor is a rare example of a 'figure of eight' racecourse. On race days punters find that the most expedient means of reaching the grandstand is by river bus.

Clewer church overlooks the old mill stream, its churchyard containing the grave of Sir Daniel Gooch, the Great Western Railway's first Loco-motive Superintendent. Equally of interest is the bowstring bridge which carries the line from Slough, for it is Brunel's work and dates from 1849. Both the Great Western and London & South Western railway companies had sought to serve Royal Windsor and win Victoria's seal of approval but Eton College had demurred, convinced that vulgar railways would undermine their pupils' morals. Towered over by the regal outlines of the world famous castle, the Thames arcs equally royally by Eton on its north bank and Windsor

to the south. The elegant cast iron (and pedestrianised) bridge which links them dates from 1824. Some fine looking restaurants abut the riverbank and it becomes difficult to resist the temptation to eat, drink and be, if not necessarily merry, at least temporarily less morose.

Romney Lock hides itself away from all the razzamatazz. The lock-keeper's cottage is demurely whitewashed and dates from 1919. There are glimpses past soaring poplars of Eton College Chapel to one side and a Victorian waterworks to the other. Black Potts railway bridge was originally designed by Joseph Locke and of considerably more ornate appearance than now. Neither can much aesthetic virtue be attached to the 1967 rebuilt version of Victoria Bridge. With stern injunctions not to moor along the Royal banks of The Home Park, the Thames flows down past Datchet's pleasant river frontage and a busy boatyard and hire base.

Eton   Map 37

An insubstantial town of great charm and history based on a handsome and lengthy High Street.

Eating & Drinking

CHRISTOPHER HOTEL - High Street. Tel: 01753 852359. Bar/grill open to non-residents. SL4 6AN
COTE BRASSERIE - High Street. Tel: 01753 868344. Mainstream French cooking from an increasingly reliable chain listed in several other locations in this guide. Grandstand view of the river. Open from 8am daily (9am Sat & Sun). SL4 6AA
GILBEY'S - High Street. Tel: 01753 854921. Endearingly smart establishment serving lunch from noon (ex Mon) and dinner from 6pm. SL4 6AF
WATERMAN'S ARMS - Brocas Street. Tel: 01753 861001. Pub adjoining Eton College Boat House. Usually at least one beer from the Windsor & Eton Brewery. SL4 6BW

Shopping

A plethora of gentlemen's outfitters with prominent displays of the College's uniforms and sports attire within their gilded windows sets the tone for Eton's exclusive High Street. Galleries and gift shops rub upstart shoulders with such illustrious establishments, but there is also a post office and a convenience store. A very good delicatessen and an antiquarian bookshop. Look out for the elegant, fluted pillar-box on the right hand side with the Thames behind you.

Things to Do

ETON COLLEGE - High Street. Tel: 01753 671177. Open to the general public between Easter and the end of September; though afternoons only during term time. A thought-provoking insight into the history of Britain's most famous school and the lifestyle of its present-day pupils. The College Chapel is worth the entry fee alone. SL4 6DW

Windsor   Map 37

Hardly anything about Windsor seems real - half Walt Disney, half *Truman Show* - and yet it attracts tourists from all over the globe; and, judging by the demeanour of some, even further afield. At the height of the tourist season, and when the flag flies over the battlements, you could be forgiven suspecting that Her Majesty is the only English person left in Windsor.

Eating & Drinking

BEL & THE DRAGON - Thames Street. Tel: 01753 866056. Thames travellers may already have encountered Bel's excellent sisters in Cookham or Reading. Bright interior and fine food. SL4 1QB
CARPENTER'S ARMS - Market Street. Tel: 01753 863739. Pub close to castle walls. Mosaic floors recall vanished Ashby's Brewery of Staines. London Pride and Doom Bar. SL4 1PB
GOGO'S - Racecourse Marina. Tel: 01753 869057. Family owned restaurant with emphasis on South African cuisine. Boat access via Bush Ait. SL6 2DW

Shopping

Peascod Street slopes down from the castle walls and boasts the main chain stores - Boots, Marks & Spencer, et al. The Windsor Royal Shopping mall is based around the grandiose Central railway station enlarged in 1897 to mark Victoria's Jubilee.

Things to Do

TOURIST INFORMATION - Central railway station. Tel: 01753 743900. Curiously reticent TIC whose staff lurk behind the grilles of the old station booking hall.
WINDSOR MUSEUM - The Guildhall. Tel: 01628 685686. Local history displays. SL4 1LR
WINDSOR CASTLE - Castle Hill. Tel: 0207 766 7304 'The oldest and largest occupied castle in the world.' SL4 1NJ

Connections

TRAINS - Great Western Railway link shuttle to Slough from Central; South-West Trains link with Datchet, Staines and Waterloo from Riverside. Tel: 0345 748 4950.

Datchet   Map 37

Public moorings render this a useful stopping-off point. Over the railway level-crossing you'll find a couple of pubs, sandwich bar and Indian and Italian restaurants. Shopping facilities include a convenience store, off licence, post office, newsagent and pharmacy. Trains run to Windsor & Eton Riverside, Staines and London Waterloo.

LIVING up to its billing as 'liquid history', the Thames flows past Runnymede and Magna Carta Island as it makes its way down from Datchet to Egham. Bad King John's run-in with the barons in 1215 might all seem like a long time ago, but the Magna Carta set precedents which still impact upon the rights of freemen throughout the democratic world.

Albert Bridge marks the southern extent of Windsor Old Park. Its elegant, balustraded profile heralds the entrance to the New Cut, dug in 1822 to obviate an extravagant bend in the river. A couple of miles to the south-east, George III's equestrian statue is prominent on Snow Hill. In truth the short-cut is rather charmless, so one welcomes the advent of Old Windsor Lock, presided over by a brick-built keeper's cottage dating from 1928.

Between the tail of Old Windsor Lock and Friary Island on the east bank of the river stands Honeypot Cottage, a quaint thatched building with three conical roofs. For many years it belonged to the much loved actress Beryl Reid and her feline retinue. The Thames here is broad and there are a number of boat-filled backwaters. Dutch barge disease appears to be spreading!

When Jerome K. Jerome alluded to the Bells of Ouseley (sic) in *Three Men In A Boat*, he was not to know that it would be hit by a German V2 rocket half a century later: it is now a Harvester restaurant. The eponymous bells are reputed to have been mislaid in the river hereabouts as they were being secretly conveyed from Osney Abbey at Oxford by monks anxious that they should be saved from Henry VIII at the time of the Dissolution.

Half a mile downstream lies French Brothers boatyard. You may be fortunate enough to catch a glimpse here of *Nuneham*, a former Salters steamer, built by Clarkes of Brimscombe on the Thames & Severn Canal

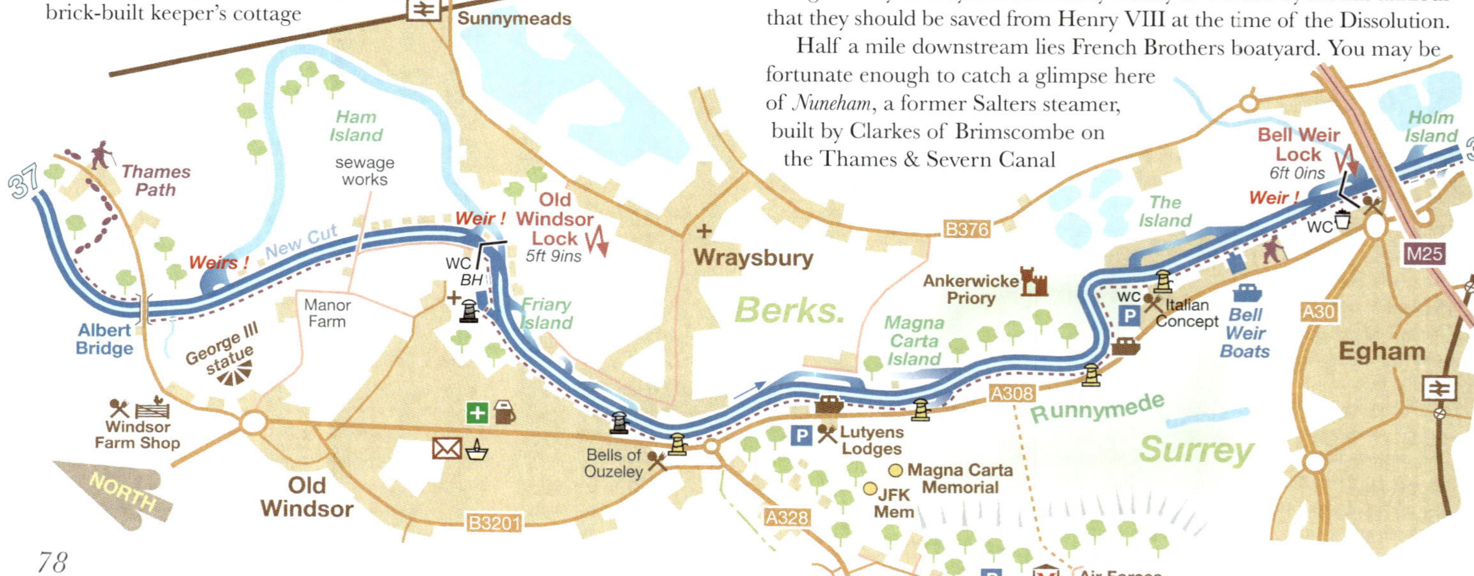

in 1898. She was converted to diesel propulsion after the Second World War and subsequently passed out of Salters fleet, eventually being acquired by French Brothers and beautifully restored to steam to mark her centenary.

French Brothers landing stage offers access to Runnymede Meadows, under the aegis now of the National Trust. Refreshments are obtainable at one of the Lutyens designed lodges or kiosks. Within easy walking distance of the riverbank are two memorials with American connotations: the Magna Carta Memorial was erected in 1957 by the American Bar Association as a symbol of freedom under law; eight years later, and less than a fortnight after the assassination of John F. Kennedy in Dallas, the British Government gifted an acre of land at Runnymede to the U.S.A. as a mark of respect in his memory. A third monument rises conspicuously above a wooded hillside to the south-west in the form of a clock tower built in 1952 and containing within its walls a sad roll call of some twenty thousand missing Commonwealth airmen. A footpath leads inexorably to the crest of the ridge from which you can visit the memorial and enjoy panoramic views across the Thames Valley.

As it flows past Runnymede, the Thames forms the boundary between Berkshire and Surrey. The keen as mustard members of Wraysbury Skiff and Punting Club put their elegant craft through their paces on this reach of the river. Bell Weir Lock lies adjacent to the notorious M25 and the traffic noise rarely dissipates. There are two bridges - arch rivals you could say - that nearest the lock having been designed by Lutyens, though erected posthumously in 1961.

Air Forces Memorial, Runnymede

Old Windsor — Map 38
Shopping
WINDSOR FARM SHOP - Datchet Road. Tel: 01753 623800. Excellent locally-sourced food outlet housed in former Windsor Estate potting shed. The accompanying coffee shop provides a good pit stop for Thames Path walkers, but boaters are denied convenient access. Open 9am-5.30pm (10am-4.30pm Sun). Memo to Her Majesty: 'Your Highness, perhaps one could give thought to the provision of mooring facilities by Albert Bridge for the benefit of one's water-borne subjects desirous of patronising one's farm shop'. SL4 2RQ

Runnymede — Map 38
Eating & Drinking
ITALIAN CONCEPT - Skytes Meadow, Windsor Road. Tel: 01784 432244. Highly regarded Italian restaurant. Closed Mons. TW20 0AE

THE LOCK - Windsor Road (adjoining Bell Weir Lock. Tel: 01784 220999. Bar and kitchen located within the Runnymede-on-Thames Hotel. TW20 0AG

A T its most bourgeois - though lent a degree of exoticism by the Rabelaisian presence of parakeets in riverside trees - the Thames slips through Staines, fulfilling the subliminal maritime fantasies of thousands of riparian dwellers. The River Colne, a confidant of Grand Union canallers, enters the Thames just below Staines Bridge, the work of Sir John Rennie, son of the more widely known canal engineer and bridge and dock builder. Here the riverside has been municipally enhanced to good effect and there are handy free moorings, whilst youngsters get a good grounding in the theories and practices of rowing. Below the railway bridge (adorned with yellow sight lines to prevent swans from flying into its unforgiving grey girders) a lych gate gives off the towpath into St Peter's Church, endowed by Sir Edward Clark KC who defended Oscar Wilde. Villas, bungalows and maisonettes characterise the waterside all the way down to Penton Hook, and notwithstanding an obvious disparity in era, an homogeneity is neatly established, near yet far neighbours regarding each other quizzically across the river where water replaces mere asphalt: one senses that the Thames lends additional subtle shades of character to those fortunate enough to dwell on its banks.

Penton Hook Lock dates from 1814 and lays claim to being the most westerly lock constructed at the behest of the City of London. Framed by horse chestnuts, the keeper's cottage is a pre-Conservancy original. It slices off a positively rococo meander of the river, the downstream portion of which leads to an extensive marina. Opposite Laleham Raw Water Intake, Laleham Boat Yard usually boasts a fine array of classic cruisers. The poet Matthew Arnold was born in Laleham and is buried in the churchyard. His almost equally famous father taught here before moving to Rugby School in 1828. Another well known Laleham family are the Lucans: one of them gave the disastrously misleading order which led to the Charge of the Light Brigade; another was a prominent activist in the early days of the Inland Waterways Association; and a third effected a celebrated disappearance.

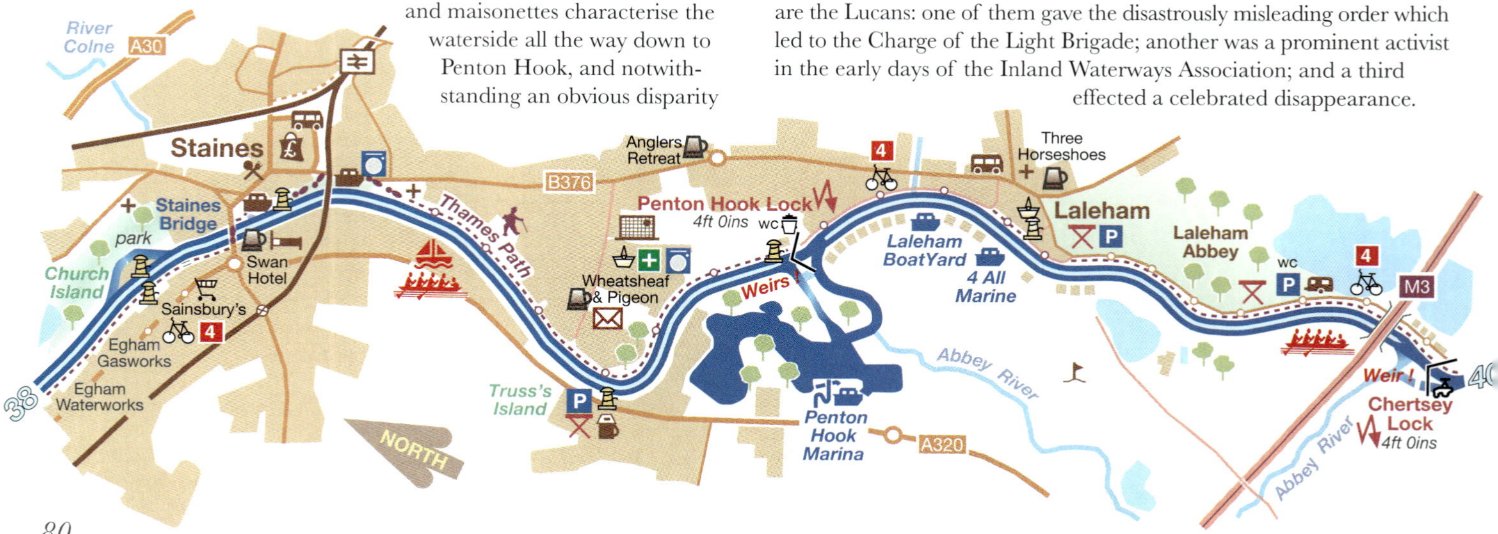

Staines-upon-Thames Map 39

Rebranded to expunge the character *stains* of 'Ali G'. The malodorous linoleum works is long gone, remembered solely by the charming statue of two men carrying a roll of that much maligned floor covering along High Street. On the wall of the elegant, Italianate Town Hall a plaque commemorates Staines' cameo role in the Battle of Trafalgar. Nelson's victory was achieved on 21st October 1805, but it took sixteen days for that news to reach the Admiralty in London. First by way of the schooner *Pickle* which docked at Falmouth on 4th November, thence by post-chaise which took 37 hours to cover the 271 miles. Its horses were changed 21 times en route, the penultimate change taking place at Staines on the evening of 5th November. A footnote in history, for sure, but an interesting item of trivia which encapsulates this proud little riverside borough's pedigree which is traceable back to Roman times.

Eating & Drinking

SUSHI NARA - High Street. Tel: 01784 558066. Town centre Japanese restaurant. TW18 4EN
THE SWAN HOTEL - The Hythe. Tel: 01784 452494. Congenial Fullers pub refurbished 2017 with customer moorings (fee redeemable at bar) and riverside patio. Good food and accommodation. TW18 3JB
WHEATSHEAF & PIGEON - Wheatsheaf Lane. Tel: 01784 452922. *Good Beer Guide* listed pub between the river and Staines Town's football ground where Chelsea Ladies also play. London Pride, Doom Bar and guests. Food ex Sun evenings. TW18 2LL

Shopping

An unexpectedly sophisticated shopping venue with two shopping malls and a cheerfully pedestrianised High Street which bustles with a market on Wednesdays. Sainsbury's occupies the site of the Lagonda motor works.

Connections

TRAINS - frequent services to/from London Waterloo and Reading, plus junction for Windsor & Eton Riverside. Tel: 0345 748 4950.
BUSES - Service 216 operates every 20 mins (30 Sun) to/from Hampton Court, providing a useful facility for Thames Path walkers. Ditto Wings service 458 which runs to/from Shepperton via Laleham half hourly (hourly Sun). Tel: 0871 200 2233.
TAXIS - Blue Star Cars. Tel: 01784 465656.

Laleham Map 39

Public moorings render this otherwise innocuous village worth considering as a stopping point with easy access to a convenience store and a smartly refurbished pub called The Three Horseshoes (Tel: 01784 455014 - TW18 1SE). Some handsome Georgian and neo-Georgian houses adorn the village green, persuading you that you are much deeper into the countryside.

CHERTSEY BRIDGE is seven-arched, finely proportioned and built of Portland stone, it dates from 1785. In recent times the setting has been somewhat compromised by the erection (downstream on the old Surrey bank) of brash, multistorey apartments. Architecturally, they may have been justifiable in some post-industrial setting nearer London, but facing Dumsey Meadow - where cattle still graze in the time-honoured manner, and where wildflowers flourish unimpeded by artificial fertilizers - they seem out of place.

A grateful nation presented Pharaoh's Island to Admiral Nelson after the Battle of the Nile. He used it, pragmatically, to fish from. Now it is home to upwards of twenty residential properties and, like true islanders, the only way for its residents to have commerce with - what passes for - civilisation is by boat. Witness them scurrying, like water-boatmen, across the surface for the post and the newspapers of a morning; most, equipped with outboards, but some sufficiently traditionally-minded to scull with a single oar. Not that commuting to and from the island is always so idyllic. As recently as 2011, two men drowned when their dinghy capsized in icy waters, feet from the bank.

A complex network of waterways surrounds Shepperton Lock, prime amongst which is the River Wey and its Navigation, navigable for some nineteen miles through Surrey (at its most leafy) to the market town of Godalming, four miles upstream of Guildford. At the tail of the lock a motorised ferry operates throughout the year, not least for the benefit of those pacing out the Thames Path, which changes sides at this point. D'Oyly Carte Island once belonged to the impresario Richard D'Oyly Carte, and on it he built the now rather elegantly faded Eyot House - Gilbert & Sullivan being frequent visitors. Desborough Cut or Channel opened in 1935 to save some three-quarters of a mile, though the original course of the river remains equally navigable. The two routes rejoin each other just upstream of Walton Bridge, rebuilt in 2013; both

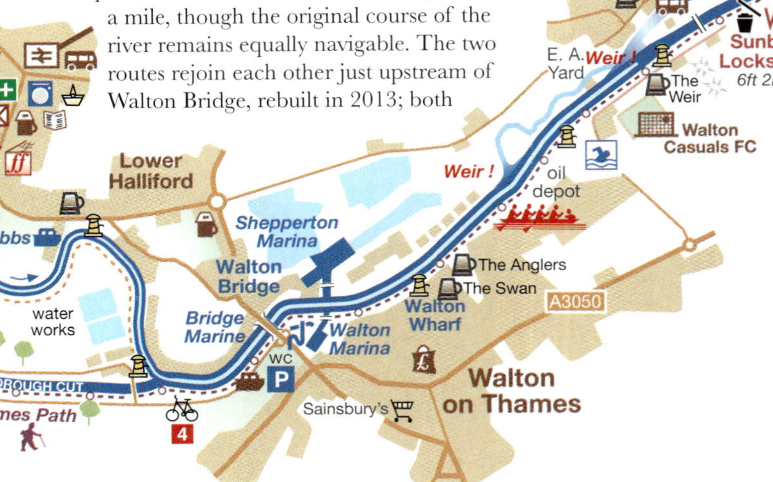

Canaletto and Turner painted earlier manifestations. Two busy marinas and a boatyard create additional levels of boating activity as the river makes its way down Walton Reach through a world of bungalows and riverside chalets bewildering in their invention and individuality. The Environment Agency, who nowadays are responsible for upkeep of the river, have a sizeable maintenance yard and drydock on the approach to Sunbury. Sunbury Locks are paired, but it is usually the southernmost (on the right heading downstream) which is used today, its older partner being still hand-operated. Like Penton Hook, it retains a pre-Thames Conservancy lock-keeper's house. On this occasion, however, a newer house, dated 1959, has supplanted the original.

Shepperton   Map 40

Famous for its film studios which are located near the giant Queen Mary Reservoir a couple of miles to the north of the river. Lower Shepperton is quaint and centred on the ancient parish church of St Nicholas. Shepperton proper is pragmatically suburban. John Gregson, who appeared in two classic British films of the Fifties, *The Titfield Thunderbolt* (see page 14) and *Genevieve*, lived at Creek House and lies buried in Sunbury Cemetery.

Eating & Drinking

THAMES COURT - riverside above Shepperton Lock. Tel: 01932 221957. Vintage Inns establishment which once belonged to the Dutch ambassador with Delft tiles to prove it. TW17 9LJ
WARREN LODGE HOTEL - Church Square. Tel: 01932 242972. Bar & restaurant meals for non-residents. TW17 9JZ

Shopping

No shops in Lower Shepperton by the river, but good facilities in Shepperton itself to the north of the B375 about quarter of an hour away. Nauticalia's maritime-themed gift shop and chandlery lies adjacent to the lock. Tel: 01932 221094. TW17 9LQ

Connections

TRAINS - terminus of outer suburban branch line from London Waterloo. Tel: 0345 748 4950. BUSES - Wings service 458 operates half hourly, (hourly Sun), between Shepperton railway station and Staines via Laleham. Tel: 0871 200 2233.
FERRY - links Shepperton with Weybridge every quarter of an hour throughout the year.

Walton on Thames   Map 40

The town centre is of blandly Sixties aspect, but the riverside is much more charming and traditional: the musical half of Gilbert & Sullivan lived at River House; elephants disembarked from barges to join travelling circuses at Walton Wharf; and (flagrantly disregarding bye-laws) Julius Caesar forded the river here in 54BC.

Eating & Drinking

THE ANGLERS - riverside by Walton Wharf. Tel: 01932 223996. Waterside gastropub. KT12 2PF
THE SWAN - Manor Row. Tel: 01932 225964. Sprawling Young's pub offering home-cooked pub food. Jerome (*Smoke Gets In Your Eyes*) Kern wooed and won the landlord's daughter here in 1910. KT12 2PF
THE WEIR - Waterside Drive. Tel: 01932 784530. Riverside pub with rooms adjacent to Sunbury Lock channel and Walton Casuals Football Club. KT12 2JB

Shopping

All the 'High Street' brands lurk in the town centre less than ten minutes walk from moorings at Walton Wharf. Large branch of Sainsbury's.

Connections

TRAINS - the railway station lies a lengthy hike to the south of the town centre. If you get that far you'll find frequent trains to/from Waterloo. Tel: 0345 748 4950.

Sunbury on Thames   Map 40

Echoes Shepperton in that it is at its prettiest beside the river, and good public moorings - approached from below Sunbury Lock - encourage waterborne visitors. A walled garden can be explored.

Eating & Drinking

LITTLE ITALY - Thames Street. Tel: 01932 787840. Characterful and authentic little Italian deli/cafe/restaurant. TW16 6AD
THE MAGPIE - Thames Street. Tel: 01932 782024. Greene King pub with riverside terrace and mooring jetty. Original meeting place of the Grand Order of Water Rats (the showbiz charity organisation) in 1889. TW16 6AF
MOON IN MOON - The Avenue. Tel: 01932 789500. Chinese restaurant. TW16 6AD
THE PHOENIX - Thames Street. Tel: 01932 785358. Cosy and welcoming pub with nice garden and customer moorings. TW16 6AF

Shopping

Useful facilities on The Avenue within easy reach of the public moorings include a cafe/bakery, small Budgens supermarket, post office, and pharmacy.

Connections

TRAINS - stop on the Shepperton branch. BUSES - Service 216 runs westwards to Staines and eastwards to Hampton, Hampton Court and Kingston. Tel: 0871 200 2233.

THE Thames flows down past Sunbury through a glittering landscape of reservoirs and water works dating from the mid-19th Century, prior to which much of the capital's drinking water was extracted from the Thames and, given the fact that it also functioned as a receptacle for sewage, cholera was unsurprisingly rife. Sunbury Court was built in the 18th Century and in recent years has been used as a conference centre by the Salvation Army. It lends its name to an island which boasts an agglomeration of chalets and bungalows, the first in a procession of 'islands in the stream' which capture your attention and engage your curiosity in almost equal measure. Platt's Eyot was the location of Thorneycroft's boatbuilding yard, its dilapidated corrugated-iron erecting sheds bear melancholy witness to a heyday which had its zenith during the First World War when motor torpedo boats were constructed here for the Admiralty. Fortunately, Molesey Lock was capacious enough to accept such vessels, having already been lengthened (to a whopping 268 feet in 1906) for the upstream coal traffic to Port Hampton. The discharged cargoes of coal were transported to the pumping stations at Hampton and Kempton (better known, of course, for its race course) by a narrow gauge railway. Much of its two foot line remains in situ and there are hopes that it may one day be resurrected as a tourist attraction. Canal aficionados may be interested to learn that its fleet of three steam locomotives hailed from the Kerr Stuart works at Stoke on Trent where L. T. C. Rolt was apprenticed.

Hampton Ferry (not to be confused with its namesake on the Avon at Evesham, let alone the ferry at Hampton Loade on the River Severn) can trace its origins back to 1514. Nowadays it operates from March to October. Prominent on the riverside stands Garrick's Shakespeare Temple, erected by the acclaimed 18th Century actor in 1773 in honour of the bard.

David Garrick purchased Hampton House in 1754 and had it rebuilt by Robert Adam. Level with Garrick's Ait on the Surrey bank stood Hurst Park Race Course which featured memorably in *Nicholas Nickleby*. One of its grandstands was burnt down by suffragettes in 1913. Upon closure of the course in 1962 its last grandstand was sold to Mansfield Town FC! Tagg's Island, now host to an eclectic flotilla of characterful houseboats, was once the base of the impresario Fred

Karno who operated a number of crowd-pleasing attractions on the islet. It was he who shipped over a complete Swiss house and had it re-erected on the Middlesex bank. It remains intact, seemingly immune to the vicissitudes of property, unlike his grandiose pleasure establishment, 'The Karsino', a magnet for the rich, famous and libidinous. Karno is variously attributed as the originator of the custard pie routine, the casting couch, and the mentor of Charlie Chaplin. The chaotic, slapstick routines which he encouraged his music hall acts to adopt gave rise to the term 'Fred Karno's Army', a title also adapted for an irreverent song sung by the troops in the trenches.

At the height of his success, Karno had an elegant houseboat built for him by a boatyard in Brentford. Launched in 1913, it was called *Astoria*, and cost more than a million in today's values. Thirteen years later he was bankrupt and ownership passed to Vesta Victoria, the comedienne who sang *Daddy Wouldn't Buy Me A Bow Wow*. Nowadays, fully restored to pristine condition, it belongs to David Gilmour of Pink Floyd and is used as an unlikely recording studio. Pink Floyd's albums *A Momentary Lapse of Reason* and *The Division Bell* along with Gilmour's own appropriately titled *On an Island* were all recorded on *Astoria*.

The civilised world is polarised into those who think of Hampton Court Palace in terms of Cardinal Wolsey and those for whom it conjures images of Harris and his chums' experience of the famous maze, as so deliciously described in *Three Men In A Boat*. Whichever set claims you, there is no escaping the Palace's impact on the river traveller. Hampton Court Bridge was designed by Sir Edward Lutyens and opened ceremoniously in 1933 by the Prince of Wales, the man who popularised the zip-fly and who was later to briefly become Edward VIII before abdicating the throne for the beguiling charms of Wallis Simpson.

Having risen romantically on the slopes of the Sussex Weald, the River Mole enters the Thames just downstream of the bridge as it glides serenely past Hampton Court Palace. The confluence is a busy spot with a number of 'steamer' piers in the vicinity. Half a mile downstream, the handsome boathouse of the Dittons Skiff & Punting Club stands on the Surrey bank; the club was founded in 1923 and is one of a number on the banks of the Thames still catering for such wonderfully arcane water sports.

Thames Ditton Island has a permanent population in excess of a hundred souls. Chalets and shanties began popping up on it early in the 20th Century, but it didn't have a permanent link to the rest of the world until a pedestrian suspension bridge joined it with the Surrey bank just before the Second World War. Many of the houses have been rebuilt more substantially but a few of the original bungalows remain to remind the island's dwellers of their more humble origins. Ferry Works on the Surrey bank houses various small businesses now, but its past output includes AC Cars and Willans & Robinsons steam reciprocating engines.

Hampton — Map 41

24 hour visitor moorings below the prominent church facilitate access to this riverine suburb of which there's more than meets the eye. You can admire the imposing waterworks architecture; take in a home game at Hampton & Richmond Borough FC; or pay homage to the Bard on Sunday afternoons between April and September when Garrick's Temple opens its door to the general public. Whilst The Bell dominates the riverscape, on Station Road there are two *Good Beer Guide* recommended pubs, restaurants, cafes and a small Waitrose at the far end.

Hampton Court — Map 41

Riverside tourist honeypot which positively hooches with visitors from all over the world all summer through. Nice walks to be enjoyed in Bushy Park where the deer tamely graze as you pass within touching distance. Ubiquitous convenience store and butcher on Bridge Street to south of bridge.

Eating & Drinking

LE PETIT NANTAIS - Bridge Road. Tel: 0208 979 2309. Terrific little French restaurant on the south bank of the river which is really East Molesey. The owner is a former French rugby international. KT8 9ER

Things to Do

HAMPTON COURT PALACE - Tel: 0333 320 6000. Sumptuous Tudor palace surrendered by Cardinal Wolsey to Henry VIII. Plus, of course, that maze! Moorings on the North bank downstream of Hampton Court Bridge provide easy access. KT8 9AU

Connections

TRAINS - terminus of outer suburban services to/from London Waterloo. Tel: 0345 748 4950. BUSES - Service 216 links Kingston with Staines and is thus extremely useful for Thames Path adventurers. Tel: 0871 200 2233.

42 RIVER THAMES Kingston & Teddington 4mls/11k/1hr

FLOWING due north past Kingston's substantial riverfront, the Thames reaches the end of its freshwater status at Teddington Locks. An obelisk, erected (downstream on the towpath side) in 1909, marks the change in responsibility for navigation between the Thames Conservancy (or these days the Environment Agency) and the Port of London Authority.

The Italianate tower of St Raphael's Catholic church looms over the riverbank on the approach to Kingston and there is a landing stage for Turks trip boat operations just before the entry of the Hogsmill River. Kingston Bridge dates from 1828 but has been progressively widened to cope with traffic demands. By 1906 it could lay claim to be the first Thames bridge to have trams running over it - would that they still were!

A massive John Lewis department store emphasises Kingston's credentials as a centre for shopping, but intrudes upon the river's propensity for avoiding harsh realities. The remains of a wharf to which tugs hauling trains of coal-laden lighters plied with fuel for the town's since demolished power station recall lost commercial trade. L. T. C. Rolt described Dutch coasting vessels delivering coal (which they had loaded from staithes on the River Tyne and carried down the East Coast) to Kingston Gasworks in his book *Thames From Mouth to Source*. But you only have to look at the adjoining railway bridge to realise that it was the dense network of lines on either bank of the Thames which brought about the demise of river traffic rather than any inherent weakness in the carriage of goods by water. By way of consolation, the railways expedited an explosion in the growth of pleasure traffic on the river. The cast iron railway bridge was built by Thomas Brassey for the London & South Western Railway in 1863. Canbury Gardens provide a soothing environment along the Surrey bank. Here, in less salubrious times, they made 'native guano', or dried human sewage for use as a manure. Inured to its noisome presence, the locals jocularly knew the gardens as 'Perfume Parade'.

The river broadens as it sweeps down to Teddington in a reach made busy by all sorts of boating activities. A hundred and thirty five miles from Lechlade,

See page 93 for notes on passage between Teddington and Brentford.

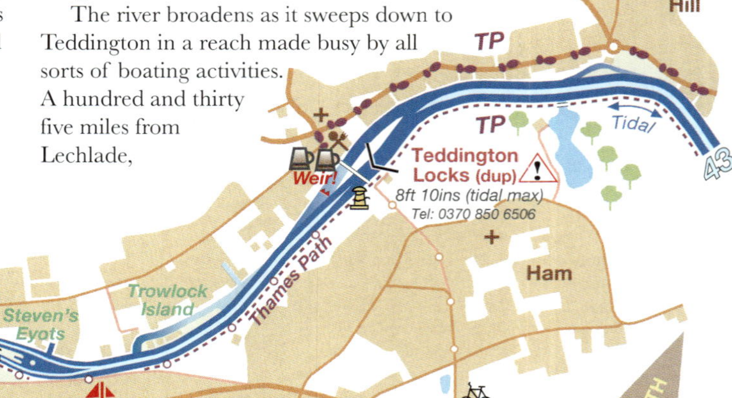

Teddington Locks mark the tidal limit of the River Thames. There are three chambers: the massive 'barge' lock dating from 1904 (650ft long x 24ft 9ins wide) which was once used by tug-hauled trains of lighters; the 'launch' lock of 1857 (177ft 11ins x 24ft 4ins); and the 'skiff' lock (49ft 6ins x 5ft 10ins). The locks are manned 24 hours per day, 365 days of the year and the friendly (if frequently busy) keepers are fountains of navigational lore. From the neighbouring Tough's Boatyard a hundred privately owned 'Little Ships' bravely set course for Dunkirk in 1940 to help in the evacuation of the British Expeditionary Force.

 The Thames Path bifurcates at Teddington offering walkers a choice of riverbanks, though initially that on the former Middlesex side deviates away from the river along suburban roads.

Thames Ditton — Map 41

Weatherboarded cottages and a flint church lend a Kentish feel to this peaceful enclave, especially when you discover that one of the best pubs is serving Shepherd Neame ales from Faversham. A shame, then, that there are not more mooring options.

Eating & Drinking
THE ALBANY - Queens Road. Tel: 0208 972 9163. Stylish riverside eating house with theatrical origins adjacent to Dittons Skiff & Punting Club premises. Mooring jetty. KT7 0QY
YE OLDE SWAN - Summer Road. Tel: 0208 398 1814. A mooring jetty is thoughtfully provided for boating customers by the suspension bridge which links Thames Ditton Island to the outside world. Roomy Greene King pub dating from the 13th Century where Henry VIII used to repair for a quiet pint. KT7 0QQ

Kingston on Thames — Map 42

Turn a blind eye to the architectural insensitivity of John Lewis' ungainly riverside store, Kingston gets much better than this once you've wended your way down its side streets and come upon the Market Place with its fine Italianate Town Hall and the anachronistic golden statue of Queen Anne. Another alley leads to the Apple Market, whence you can come full circle to Clatten Bridge which spans the Hogsmill River and is thought to derive its name from the sound of horses hooves.

Eating & Drinking
AL FORNO - Townsend Parade. Tel: 0208 439 7555. Atmospheric Italian open for lunch and dinner Mon-Thur and from noon Fri-Sun. KT1 1LY
BISHOP OUT OF RESIDENCE - Riverside. Tel: 020 8546 4965. Plush modern Youngs pub serving food from 10am to 10.30pm. KT1 1PY
BOATERS INN - Canbury Gardens. Tel: 0208 541 4672. Lively riverside bar which originated as a municipal tea room. Limited customer moorings during opening hours. KT2 5AU
COTE - Riverside Walk. Tel: 0208 546 9422. Robust French chain restaurant with Thames-side views. Open from 8am (9am weekends). KT1 1QN
HARTS BOATYARD - Portsmouth Road. Tel: 0208 399 7515. Riverside pub and dining room. KT6 4HL
LAS IGUANAS - High Street. Tel: 0208 546 2245. Zany Latin American chain restaurant. KT1 1LL

Shopping
Kingston offers excellent and enjoyable shopping facilities which range from the hauteur of Bentalls and John Lewis' department stores to the magnanimity of the Market Square, and these are easily accessed by boaters from good moorings on the Middlesex bank upstream of Kingston Bridge. The town's vibrant Ancient Market functions Mon-Sat, and in addition there's a specialist Monday Market. On Old London Road (marked by a street sculpture of falling over red telephone boxes) there's a cheerful mix of niche shops.

Connections
TRAINS - Kingston loop services to/from London Waterloo with useful link with Shepperton for Thames Path walks. Tel: 0345 748 4950.
TAXIS - Kingston Black Cab. Tel: 0208 546 1993.

Teddington — Map 42

Teddington Studios (now being converted into apartments) could trace their origins back to the dawn of film-making. Many British feature films were made here in the 1930s, but the studios were destroyed by a V1 rocket in 1944, and did not return to full production until four years later when they were formally re-opened by Danny Kaye. In the Sixties and Seventies the studios enjoyed a heyday in the making of television programmes such as *The Avengers*, *Minder* and *The Benny Hill Show*. When The Beatles arrived here by boat in 1964 to appear on Mike & Bernie Winters' *Big Night Out* a teenage fan broke through security. When George Harrison asked her what she wanted, she immortally replied: "I Wanna Hold Your Hand."

Eating & Drinking
THE ANGLERS - Broom Road. Tel: 0208 977 7475. Fullers bar/dining room with large riverside garden, open from noon for food daily. TW11 9NR
THE WHARF - Manor Road. Tel: 0208 977 6333. Smart bar/restaurant with good views overlooking Teddington Lock. Closed Mondays. TW11 8BG

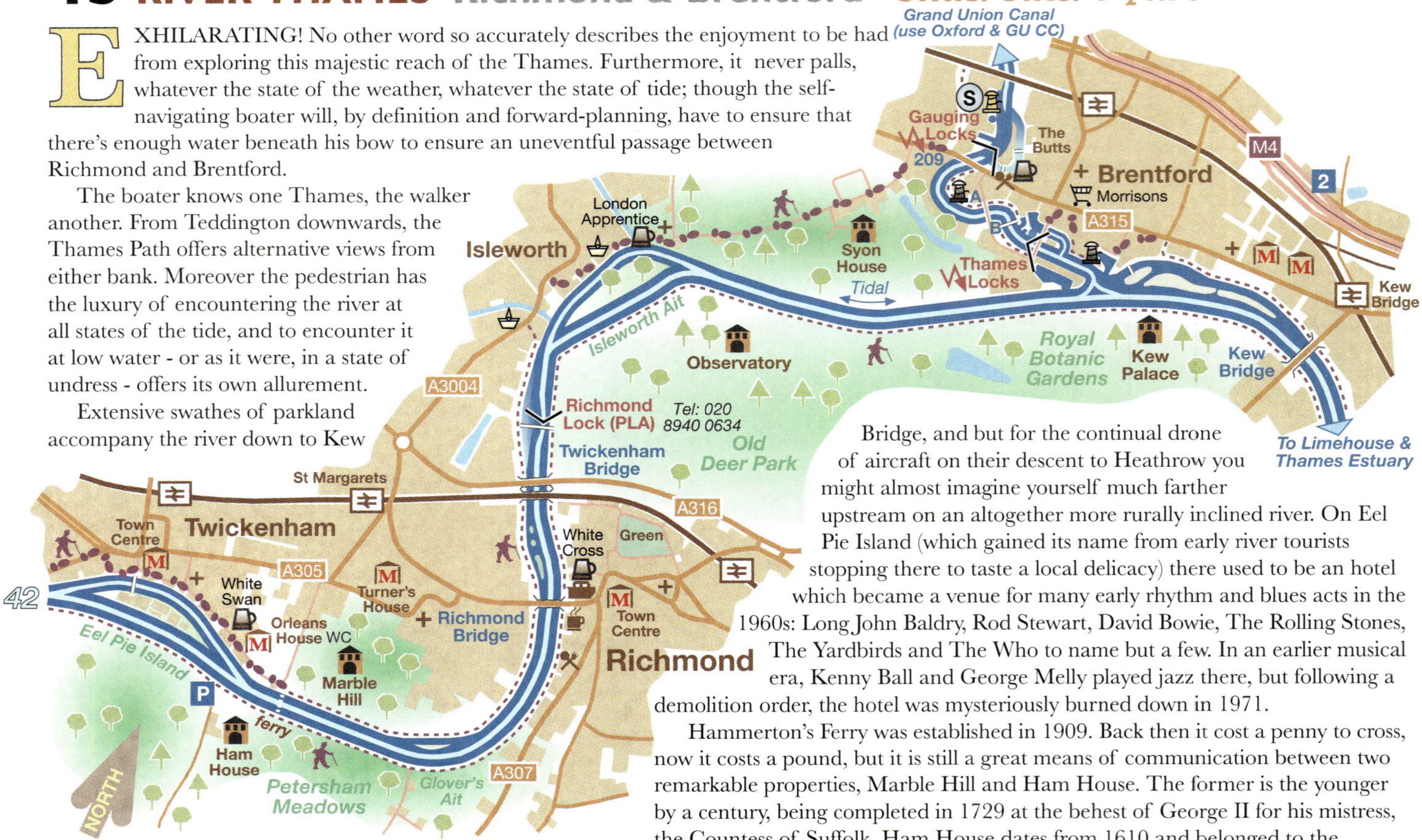

EXHILARATING! No other word so accurately describes the enjoyment to be had from exploring this majestic reach of the Thames. Furthermore, it never palls, whatever the state of the weather, whatever the state of tide; though the self-navigating boater will, by definition and forward-planning, have to ensure that there's enough water beneath his bow to ensure an uneventful passage between Richmond and Brentford.

The boater knows one Thames, the walker another. From Teddington downwards, the Thames Path offers alternative views from either bank. Moreover the pedestrian has the luxury of encountering the river at all states of the tide, and to encounter it at low water - or as it were, in a state of undress - offers its own allurement.

Extensive swathes of parkland accompany the river down to Kew

Bridge, and but for the continual drone of aircraft on their descent to Heathrow you might almost imagine yourself much farther upstream on an altogether more rurally inclined river. On Eel Pie Island (which gained its name from early river tourists stopping there to taste a local delicacy) there used to be an hotel which became a venue for many early rhythm and blues acts in the 1960s: Long John Baldry, Rod Stewart, David Bowie, The Rolling Stones, The Yardbirds and The Who to name but a few. In an earlier musical era, Kenny Ball and George Melly played jazz there, but following a demolition order, the hotel was mysteriously burned down in 1971.

Hammerton's Ferry was established in 1909. Back then it cost a penny to cross, now it costs a pound, but it is still a great means of communication between two remarkable properties, Marble Hill and Ham House. The former is the younger by a century, being completed in 1729 at the behest of George II for his mistress, the Countess of Suffolk. Ham House dates from 1610 and belonged to the matrimonially more fastidious Earl of Lauderdale.

The Thames bends majestically past Glover's Ait overlooked by the former Star & Garter home for disabled servicemen, converted into luxury apartments in 2015. Richmond's riverfront is graciously neo-classical. Its bridge dates from 1777 and is palpably one of the prettiest on the Thames. Given the semi-tidal status of the river at this point, the plying of trip boats, and the rowing boats and skiffs which one can hire, there is a maritime atmosphere about Richmond's elegant river frontage; though, paradoxically, no formal provision for visitor moorings.

In common with Black Potts Bridge at Windsor, Richmond railway bridge was designed by Joseph Locke in 1848, and was strengthened sixty years later by the Horseley Iron Works of BCN fame. Cheek by jowl it spans the Thames alongside the ferro-concrete simplicity of Twickenham Bridge, opened by the Prince of Wales on the very same day in 1933 that he cut the tape on the new bridges at Hampton Court (Map 41) and Chiswick - one trusts he had a good attention *span*!

Controlled by the Port of London Authority, Richmond Lock maintains a minimum depth of water of five feet nine inches in the reach upstream as far as Teddington. Two hours after High Water, sluices are lowered into the river to create this artificial depth. They remain in place until two hours before the next High Water, and during the intervening period, passing vessels are obliged to use the lock at the cost of a fiver. During the period when the sluices are raised, boats may pass beneath them unhindered. Navigational matters notwithstanding, Richmond Lock is a handsome aggregate of ornate Victorian kiosks and cabins which would not look out of place on the front at Brighton or Eastbourne. As with Teddington, Richmond Lock is manned (in the modern parlance) 'twenty-four/seven'.

Skirting Old Deer Park - where fledgling rugby internationals were played before Twickenham was opened in 1909 - the Thames, now prone to significant fluctuations in level, runs northwards in the direction of Brentford. Two strands of the River Crane enter the Thames at either end of willowy, heron-haunted Isleworth Ait. The picturesque Pavilion Boat House provides a precursor to Syon House, a stately pile dating largely from the 16th Century with interiors by Robert Adam, and now a hugely popular visitor attraction. Were its gracious demesne not sufficiently alluring, the opposite bank of the Thames skirts the Royal Botanic Gardens at Kew. And so it is by being book-ended between two of Greater London's most revered properties, that our coverage of the Thames comes to its conclusion at Brentford. Downstream - past a trio of heron-nested, live-aboard barge-haunted eyots - lies Kew Bridge, Central London and the sea, but for those voyaging between the river and the canal system, or vice versa, Brentford is a border post which needs to be negotiated with a degree of foresight and care.

The Great Western Railway's once extensive Brentford Dock (which ceased functioning towards the end of the Sixties, thereafter being converted into housing, though a private mooring basin remains) acts as a useful landmark to port (left) for the downstream boater intent on turning off the Thames to join the canal system. Acute the angle may be, but there is plenty of room to manoeuvre, and straight ahead lie the welcoming arms of the duplicated and manned (at, or either side of, high water) Thames Locks. Navigation requires concentration, but there is much to see and savour: weir channels, arms and backwaters where the maintenance of boats is a surviving art. And though technically once through the locks you are on the Grand Union Canal, this is really the River Brent.

Bridge 209A used to carry the railway into Brentford Dock, but whilst it is a long time since trains of lighters congregated on the flood tide to negotiate the locks up onto the Grand Union Canal, a latent, post-industrial ambience remains, and can palpably be embraced by those in tune with the past. Encountering a further gallimaufry of residential craft, you reach the Gauging Locks, automated, paired and boater-operated by a contol panel located on the central island between the two chambers. Above them lie visitor moorings and boater facilities couched in a 21st century environment of hotels and bars. To expedite informed progress up the Grand Union, acquire a copy of *Pearson's Canal Companion to the Oxford & Grand Union Canals*.

Richmond
Map 43

Originally known as Sheen, but renamed by Henry VII after his Dukedom in Yorkshire, Richmond beams so beguilingly down upon the Thames that passing boaters can only be frustrated by the lack of formal visitor moorings. For Thames Path walkers there is no alibi for not stopping. There is much to admire and to enjoy, and visitors can graduate from Richmond Green to Richmond Hill with growing appreciation for a handsome town which should never mistakenly be consigned to oblivion as a mere satellite of the capital.

Eating & Drinking
AL BOCCON DI' VINO - Red Lion Street. Tel: 0208 940 9060. Marvellous Italian open for lunch Thur-Sun and dinner Tue-Sun. TW9 1RW

STEIN'S - Riverside. Tel: 0203 746 6240. The fact that Richmond's German sizeable community frequents this Bavarian restaurant and beer garden bodes well for its authenticity. Well-appointed waterside tables, German beers and wines, and the best wurst this side of Wiesbaden. TW10 6UX

TIDE TABLES - Richmond Bridge. Tel: 0208 948 8285. Charming vegetarian (vegan and gluten-free) cafe with waterside terrace. TW9 1TH

Shopping
Excellent shopping centre with some fine independent retailers. King Street is rich in quirky, off-beat outlets, as are Paved Court and Brewers Lane; the latter playing host to Danieli's which dispenses freshly-made Italian ice cream.

Things to Do
MUSEUM OF RICHMOND - Old Town Hall. Tel: 0208 332 1141. TW9 1TP

RIVER THAMES VISITOR CENTRE - floating river lore. Tel: 0208 940 7500. TW10 6UJ

Connections
TRAINS - services to/from London Waterloo and also the westernmost terminus of the useful North London Line and the District Line. Tel: 0345 748 4950.

Twickenham
Map 43

Synonymous with rugby football worldwide, Twickenham away from its stadium resembles a smaller version of Richmond, but similarly lacks formal visitor mooring facilities - though Hammerton's Ferry may be able to squeeze you onto their pontoon at a pinch. Look out for the 'naked ladies' in York House Gardens, a collection of Carrara marble nymphs.

Eating & Drinking
THE WHITE SWAN - Riverside. Tel: 0208 744 2951. Charming waterside inn with terrace overlooking pebbly 'beach' at low tide. TW1 3DN

Shopping
Church Street hosts an array of characterful shops, whilst elsewhere most practical needs are met.

Things to Do
ORLEANS HOUSE GALLERY - Riverside. Tel: 0208 831 6000. Tue-Sun, 10am-5pm. TW1 3BL

TURNER'S HOUSE - Sandycombe Road. Tel: 0208 892 5485. The incomparable painter's self-designed villa is now open to the public. TW1 2LR

TWICKENHAM MUSEUM - The Embankment. Tel: 0208 408 0070. Local history in former waterman's cottage, including much of riverine import. Open Tue & Sat 11am-3pm, Sundays 2-4pm. TW1 3DU

Isleworth
Map 43

Idyllic Thameside settlement. Vincent Van Gogh lived, taught and preached here briefly in 1876. All Saints riverside church retains its 14th century tower, but the bulk of the building dates from the 1970s, the nave having been destroyed by arson during WWII.

Eating & Drinking
LONDON APPRENTICE - Church Street. Tel: 0208 560 1915. *Good Beer Guide* listed waterside pub. Henry VIII used it for assignations with Catherine Howard and Charles II with Nell Gwynne. TW7 6BG

Brentford
Map 43

Once the administrative centre of that forgotten county Middlesex, redevelopment of Brentford marches remorselessly on, but there are pockets of an older Brentford here and there, not least The Butts, a charming backwater behind the Market Place where stands the former Canal Boatman's Institute.

Eating & Drinking
SIRACUSA - Brentford Lock. Tel: 0208 758 0998. Italian overlooking Gauging Locks. TW8 8LF

THE WEIR - Market Place. Tel: 0208 568 3600. Sophisticated bar and eating place with a fine garden backing on to the River Brent. Interestingly, the artist Turner stayed here as a boy circa 1785. TW8 8EQ

Shopping
All facilities in High Street, including a Morrisons supermarket at its easterly end.

Things to Do
LONDON MUSEUM OF WATER AND STEAM - Green Dragon Lane. Tel: 0208 568 4757. Superb museum housed in 19th century waterworks dominated by ornate tower chimney. TW8 0EW

SYON HOUSE & PARK - Tel: 0208 560 0882. 17th Century home of the Dukes of Northumberland, 5 minutes walk from Gauging Locks and Visitor Moorings. TW8 8JG

Connections
TRAINS - frequent services on the Hounslow Loop to/from London Waterloo and Staines (change for Windsor, Reading etc). Tel: 0345 748 4950.

This Guide

Pearson's Canal Companions are a long established, independently produced series of guide books devoted to the inland waterways and designed to appeal equally to boaters, walkers, cyclists and other, less readily pigeon-holed members of society. Considerable pride is taken to make these guides as up to date, accurate, entertaining and inspirational as possible. A good guide book should fulfil three functions: make you want to go; interpret the lie of the land when you're there; and provide a lasting souvenir of your journeys. It is to be hoped that this guide ticks all three boxes, and possibly more besides.

The Maps

There are forty-three numbered maps whose layout is shown by the Route Planner inside the front cover. Maps 1 to 21 cover the Kennet & Avon between Bristol and Reading; Maps 22 to 43 cover the River Thames between Oxford and Brentford.

The maps - measured imperially like the waterways they depict, and not being slavishly north-facing - are easily read in either direction. Users will thus find most itineraries progressing smoothly and logically from left to right or vice versa. Figures quoted at the top of each map refer to distance per map, locks per map and average cruising time.

An alternative indication of timings from centre to centre can be found on the Route Planner. Obviously, cruising times vary with the nature of your boat and the number of crew at your disposal, so quoted times should be taken only as an estimate. Neither do times quoted take into account any delays which might occur at lock flights in high season or against strong current conditions on the river sections. Walking and cycling times will depend very

INFORMATION

much on the state of individual sections of towpath and the stamina of those concerned.

The Text

Each map is accompanied by a route commentary placing the waterway in its historic, social and topographical context. As close to each map as is feasible, gazetteer-like entries are given for places passed through, listing facilities of significance to users of this guide. Every effort is made to ensure these details are as up to date as possible, but - especially where pubs/restaurants are concerned - we suggest you telephone ahead if relying upon an entry to provide you with a meal at any given time.

Walking

The simplest way to explore the inland waterways is on foot along towpaths originally provided so that horses could 'tow' boats. Walking costs little more than the price of shoe leather and you are free to concentrate on the passing scene; something that boaters, with the responsibilities of navigation thrust upon them, are not always at liberty to do. The maps set out to give some idea of the quality of the towpath on any given section of canal. More of an art than a science to be sure, but at least it reflects our personal experiences, and whilst it does vary from area to area, none of it should prove problematical for anyone inured to the vicissitudes of country walking.

We recommend the use of public transport to facilitate 'one-way' itineraries but stress the advisability

of checking up to date details on the telephone numbers quoted, or on the websites of National Rail Enquiries or Traveline for trains and buses respectively. The towpath on the Kennet & Avon Canal is in walkable condition throughout, though inclined to be gluey after rain where it has not been upgraded for use as a cycleway. Furthermore, in its passage through the Kennet Valley, sections of the towpath can prove impassable at times of flood.

Walking beside rivers is not always so easy. Over the centuries landowners have appropriated many ancient rights of way, whilst the demise of former ferries has also broken links which once existed.

The River Avon Trail follows the Bristol Avon closely between Bristol and Bath. Much of the way it is well-surfaced, though in parts it remains merely a field path: *www.riveravontrail.org.uk*.

The Thames Path is a 184 mile long distance path following the river from its source in Gloucestershire to the Thames Barrier in East London. Between Oxford and Brentford it mostly follows the old towing path except for one or two places where former ferries have ceased to function: *www.nationaltrail.co.uk*

As reliable as we trust this guide will be, the additional use of an up to date Ordnance Survey Landranger or Explorer sheet is recommended as they are able to present your chosen route in a broader context. Should you be considering walking the full length of these paths over several consecutive days, Tourist Information Centres can usually be relied upon to offer accommodation advice.

Cycling

Bicycling along towpaths is an increasingly popular pastime, though one not always equally popular with other waterway users such as boaters, anglers and pedestrians. It is important to remember that you are sharing the towpath with other people out for their own form of enjoyment, and to treat them with the respect and politeness they deserve. A bell is a useful form of diplomacy; failing that, a stentorian cough. Happily, since the inception of the Canal & River Trust, it is no longer necessary for cyclists to acquire a permit to use the towpath. The Kennet & Avon towpath is utilised as National Cycle Route No.4 between Bath and Devizes and Marsh Benham (just west of Newbury) and Reading (though in the latter case there are one or two diversions away from the towpath) and the surface has been significantly and admirably enhanced with this in mind. Cycling beside the Avon and Thames (upstream of Runnymede) rivers is not formally encouraged, and the surface of their riverbank towpaths is often unsuitable for bicycling with any degree of comfort.

Boating

Boating on inland waterways is an established, though relatively small, facet of the UK tourist industry. It is also, increasingly, a chosen lifestyle. There are approximately 35,000 privately owned boats registered on the inland waterways, but in addition to these, numerous firms offer boats for hire. These range from small operators with half a dozen boats to sizeable fleets run by companies with several bases.

Most hire craft have all the creature comforts you are likely to expect. In the excitement of planning a boating holiday you may give scant thought to the contents of your hire boat, but at the end of a hard day's boating such matters take on more significance, and a well equipped, comfortable boat, large enough to accommodate your crew with something to spare, can make the difference between a good holiday and one which will be shudderingly remembered for the wrong reasons.

Traditionally, hire boats are booked out by the week or fortnight, though many firms now offer more flexible short breaks or extended weeks. All reputable hire firms give newcomers tuition in boat handling and lock working, and first-timers soon adapt to the pace of things 'on the cut' or on the river.

Navigational Advice

Newcomers, hiring a boat on the inland waterways for the first time, have every right to expect sympathetic and thorough tuition from the company providing their boat. Boat-owners are, by definition, likely to be already adept at navigating. The following, however, may prove useful points of reference.

Locks are part of the charm of inland waterway cruising, but they can be potentially dangerous environments for children, pets and careless adults. Use of them should be methodical and unhurried, whilst special care should be exercised in rain, frost and snow when slippery hazards abound. We lack space for detailed instructions on lock operation: trusting that if you own your own boat you will already be experienced in canal cruising; whilst first-time hire boaters should be given tuition in the operation of locks before they set out.

The locks included in this guide are all of the widebeam variety and capable of accepting two narrowboats side by side. On the Kennet & Avon Canal they are boater operated. Similarly on the River Avon, though there is a lock-keeper at Netham and sometimes at Hanham. On some sections of the Kennet & Avon Canal boaters are asked to leave the locks empty after use.

On the River Thames all the locks are mechanised and either manned or 'self-service' boater operated. When waiting to use a lock, form an orderly queue at the layby provided. When the lock gates open keep alert for instructions from the keeper who may, for reasons of efficiency and/or safety, require boats to enter the lock in a specific order. Once inside the lock you should secure lines fore and aft, keeping them fairly taut as the level rises or falls. Powered boats should switch their engines off whilst in the lock chamber. Finally, it behoves us all to be on our best behaviour at locks. Remember to exercise a little 'give and take'. The use of aggression to decide precedence at locks is one inland waterway tradition not worthy of preservation.

Movable bridges - which either lift or swing - are encountered in a number of locations on the Kennet & Avon Canal. Some are 'hand-operated', some are mechanised, particularly where public roads are concerned. Try to be as courteous as possible to road users, they tend to lack the inland waterway users reservoirs of patience.

Mooring on the canals featured in this guide is per usual practice - ie on the towpath side, away from sharp bends, bridge-holes and narrows. A 'yellow' bollard symbol represents visitor mooring sites; either as designated officially or, in some cases as recommended by our personal experience.

On rivers mooring is usually more problematical, the banks are not always even, there are shallows to contend with, and frequently the riparian rights are privately owned. Thus, cruising the rivers Avon and Thames requires careful planning. We have indicated on the maps the best known sites. Where these are municipally or privately owned there is often a fee to pay - though not always collected! Overnight mooring is available at many Thames locks at the discretion of the lock-keeper. Thames Visitor Moorings (Tel: 01932 506131) is a useful internet based facility for finding and booking (and paying for, where necessary) moorings along the river. Boaters should not moor where expressly forbidden, for to do so will only cause aggravation and give the inland waterways a bad name.

Turning points on the canals are known as 'winding holes'; pronounced as the thing which blows because in the old days the wind was expected to do much of the work rather than the boatman. Winding holes capable of taking a full length boat of around seventy foot length are marked where appropriate on the maps. Winding holes capable of turning shorter craft are marked with the approximate length. It is of course possible to turn boats at junctions and at most boatyards, though in the case of the latter it is considered polite to seek permission to do so.

Boating facilities are provided at regular intervals along the inland waterways, and range from a simple water tap or refuse disposal skip, to the provision of sewage disposal, showers and laundry. Such vital features are also obtainable at boatyards and marinas along with repairs and servicing. An alphabetical list of boatyards appears on pages 94 & 95.

Closures (or 'stoppages' in canal parlance) traditionally occur on the inland waterways between November and April, during which time most of the heavy maintenance work is undertaken. Occasionally, however, an emergency stoppage, or perhaps water restriction, may be imposed at short notice, closing part of the route you intend to use. Up to date details are available on *www.canalrivertrust.org.uk* or from hire bases. On the River Thames details of maintenance closures can be obtained by telephoning 0345 988 1188 - when prompted press 1 followed by 011132.

Brentford to/from Teddington

Boaters making their way along the tidal Thames between Teddington Locks and Brentford Gauging Locks need to plan ahead. Thames Locks at Brentford are only open at specific states of the tide and use of them needs to be booked in advance by telephoning 0303 040 4040. CRT publish a *Tidal Locks Availability* leaflet which can be obtained from their London Office - see column three.

Passage between Teddington and Brentford takes approximately one and a quarter hours and to make the best of the ebb tide you should plan to pass through Teddington Lock half an hour before high water. In the opposite direction plan to leave Brentford about two hours before high water and your passage upstream will have the benefit of the flow. Teddington Lock can be contacted on 0370 850 6506.

Strictly speaking, all craft using the tidal Thames should be equipped with VHF radio. However, canal-based craft travelling solely between Brentford and Teddington are deemed exempt as long as the Port of London Authority are advised on departure and arrival by telephoning 0208 855 0315.

Societies

The Inland Waterways Association was founded in 1946 to campaign for the retention of the canal system. Many routes now open to pleasure boaters may not have been so but for this organisation. Membership details, together with details of the IWA's regional branches, may be obtained from: Inland Waterways Association, Island House, Moor Road, Chesham HP5 1WA. Tel: 01494 783453. *www.waterways.org.uk*

The Kennet & Avon Canal Trust was formed in 1962 with the object of restoring the canal to full navigation. You can join the Trust by contacting them at: Kennet & Avon Canal Trust, Devizes Wharf, Couch Lane, Devizes, Wilts SN10 1EB. Tel: 01380 721279 *www.katrust.org*

The River Thames Society (also formed in 1962) protects and promotes the Thames from source to sea. They can be contacted at 23a Cuxham Road, Watlington OX49 5JW. Tel: 01461 612456.

Useful Contacts

CANAL & RIVER TRUST

www.canalrivertrust.org.uk
Kennet & Avon Waterways, The Locks, Bath Road, Devizes, Wiltshire SN10 1QR Tel: 0303 040 4040.
London Waterways, 420 Manchester Road, London E14 9ST Tel: 0303 040 4040.

RIVER THAMES

Environment Agency, Kings Meadow House, Kings Meadow Road, Reading RG1 8DQ Tel: 0370 850 6506. *www.visitthames.co.uk*
Port of London Authority, Royal Pier Road, Gravesend, Kent DA12 2BG Tel: 01474 562200. *www.boatingonthethames.co.uk*

BRISTOL HARBOUR

Underfall Yard, Cumberland Road, Bristol BS1 6XG Tel: 0117 903 1484 *www.bristol.gov.uk*

Acknowledgements

Much (alphabetical) appreciation to: Keith Goss, Meg Gregory, David Hymers, Jackie Pearson, all at the Short Run Press of Exeter, Karen Tanguy, and Jenny Tyte.

Hire Bases

ABC BOAT HIRE - Hilperton, Kennet & Avon, Map 6; Aldermaston, Kennet & Avon, Map 19. PO Box 232, Worcester WR1 2SD. Tel: 0808 291 4106 www.abcboathire.com

ANGLO WELSH WATERWAY HOLIDAYS - Bath, Map 4; Bradford-on-Avon, Map 5. 2 The Hide Market, West Street, Bristol BS2 0BH Tel: 0117 304 1122 www.anglowelsh.co.uk

BATH CANAL BOAT CO. - Bath, Kennet & Avon, Map 4. Darlington Wharf, Beckford Road, Bath BA2 6NJ Tel: 01225 312935 www.bathcanalboats.co.uk

BLACK PRINCE HOLIDAYS - Bradford on Avon, Kennet & Avon, Map 5. Stoke Prior, Bromsgrove B60 4LA Tel: 01527 575115 www.black-prince.com

THE BRUCE TRUST - boat hire for the disabled from bases at Gt Bedwyn (Map 13) and Foxhangers (Map 8). Tel: 0778 972 7493 www.brucetrust.org.uk

CAVERSHAM BOAT SERVICES - Reading, River Thames, Map 30. The Boat House, Fry's Island, Reading RG1 8DG Tel: 0118 957 4323 www.cavershamboatservices.co.uk

COLLEGE CRUISERS - Oxford, Oxford Canal, Map 22. Combe Road, Oxford OX2 6BL Tel: 01865 554343 www.collegecruisers.com

FOXHANGERS MARINE - Devizes, Kennet & Avon Canal, Map 8. Lower Foxhangers, Devizes, Wiltshire SN10 1SS Tel: 01380 827808 www.foxhangers.co.uk

HOBBS OF HENLEY - Henley, River Thames, Map 32. Station Road, Henley-on-Thames RG9 1AZ Tel: 01491 572035 www.hobbsofhenley.com

HONEYSTREET BOATS - Honeystreet, Kennet & Avon, Map 10. Honeystreet, Pewsey SN9 5PS Tel: 01672 851166 www.honeystreetboats.co.uk

BOATING DIRECTORY

KRIS CRUISERS - Datchet, River Thames, Map 37. The Waterfront, Southlea Road, Datchet, Berkshire SL3 9BU Tel: 01753 543930 www.kriscruisers.co.uk

LE BOAT - Benson, River Thames, Map 26. Waterfront, Benson, Oxfordshire OX10 6SJ Tel: 01491 824067 www.leboat.com

MOONRAKER - Honeystreet, Kennet & Avon, Map 10. Honeystreet Wharf, Wilts SN9 5PS Tel: 01672 851550 www.moonboats.co.uk

MY RIVER CRUISING - Reading, River Thames, Map 30. Caversham, Reading RG4 5BS. Tel: 0778 088 7172 www.myrivercruising.com

SALLY NARROWBOATS - Bradford-on-Avon, Kennet & Avon Canal, Map 5. Bradford Marina, Trowbridge Road, Bradford-on-Avon, Wiltshire BA15 1UD Tel: 01225 864923 www.sallynarrowboats.co.uk

WHITE HORSE BOATS - Devizes, Kennet & Avon Canal, Map 8. Burbage Wharf, Burbage SN8 3BJ Tel: 01672 810634 www.whitehorsenarrowboats.co.uk

WILTSHIRE NARROWBOATS - Bradford Wharf, Kennet & Avon Canal, Map 5. BA15 2EA. Tel: 01225 863987 www.wiltshire-narrowboats.co.uk

Boatyards

4 ALL MARINE - Laleham, River Thames, Map 39. Tel: 01932 567744. KT16 8RP

ABINGDON BRIDGE MARINE - Abingdon, River Thames, Map 24. Tel: 01235 521125. OX14 3HX

ALDERMASTON WHARF - Aldermaston, Kennet & Avon, Map 19. Tel: 0118 971 4123. RG7 4JS

BATH NARROW BOATS - Sydney Wharf, Bath, Kennet & Avon, Map 4. Tel: 01225 447276. BA2 4EL

BATH MARINA - Newbridge, River Avon, Map 3. Tel: 01225 424301. BS1 3JT

BATES WHARF - Chertsey, River Thames, Map 40. Tel: 01932 571141. KT16 8LG

BELL WEIR BOATS - Egham, River Thames, Map 38. Tel: 0795 879 2122. TW20 0AB

BETTER BOATING - Reading, River Thames, Maps 21 & 30. Tel: 0118 947 9536. RG4 8EX

(THE) BOATYARD - Hilperton, Kennet & Avon Canal, Map 6. Tel: 01225 710017. BA14 8RS

BOURNE END MARINA - Bourne End, River Thames, Map 35. Tel: 01628 522813. SL8 5RR

BRADFORD-ON-AVON MARINA - Bradford-on-Avon, Kennet & Avon Canal, Map 5. Tel: 01225 864562. BA15 1UD

BRADFORD WHARF - Bradford-on-Avon, Kennet & Avon Canal, Map 5. Tel: 0797 579 9994. BA15 2EA

BRAY MARINA (MDL) - Bray, River Thames, Map 36. Tel: 01628 623654. SL6 2EB

BRISTOL BOATS - Saltford Lock, River Avon, Map 3. Tel: 01225 872032. BS31 3ER

BRISTOL MARINA - Bristol, River Avon, Map 1. Tel: 0117 921 3198. BS1 6UH

BUSHNELLS - Wargrave, River Thames, Map 31. Tel: 0118 940 2162. RG10 8HB

CAEN HILL MARINA - Rowde, Kennet & Avon Canal, Map 8. Tel: 01380 827062. SN10 1SS

CAVERSHAM BOAT SERVICES - Reading, River Thames, Maps 21 & 30. Tel: 0118 957 4323. RG1 8DG

CHERTSEY MEADS MARINE - Chertsey, River Thames, Map 40. Tel: 01932 564699. KT16 8LN

D. B. MARINE - Cookham, River Thames, Map 35. Tel: 01628 526032. SL6 9SN

DEVIZES MARINA VILLAGE - Devizes, Kennet & Avon Canal, Map 8. Tel: 01380 725300. SN10 2RH

DRIVELINE MARINE - Tilehurst, River Thames, Map 29. Tel: 0118 942 3877. RG30 6AY

FOXHANGER WHARF - Foxhangers, Kennet & Avon Canal, Map 8. Tel: 01380 827808. SN10 1SS

FROUDS BRIDGE MARINA - Aldermaston, Kennet & Avon Canal, Map 18. Tel: 0118 971 4508. RG7 4LH

GIBBS MARINE - Shepperton, River Thames, Map 40. Tel: 01932 242977. TW17 9HY

HAMBLEDEN MILL MARINA - Mill End, River Thames, Map 33. Tel: 01491 571316. RG9 3AY

HARLEYFORD MARINA - Harleyford, River Thames, Map 34. Tel: 01628 471361. SL7 2DX

HARTS BOATYARD - Surbiton, River Thames, Map 42. Tel: 0208 399 0297. KT6 4HJ

HILPERTON MARINA - Hilperton, Kennet & Avon Canal, Map 6. Tel: 01225 765243. BA14 8RS

HOBBS & SONS - Henley on Thames, River Thames, Map 32. Tel: 01491 572035. RG9 1AZ

HONEYSTREET WHARF - Honeystreet, Kennet & Avon Canal, Map 10. Tel: 01672 851550. SN9 5PS

KRIS CRUISERS - Datchet, River Thames, Map 37. Tel: 01753 543930. SL3 9BU

LINDON LEWIS MARINE - Shepperton, River Thames, Map 40. Tel: 01932 247427. TW17 8NS

NEWBURY BOAT COMPANY - Newbury, Kennet & Avon, Map 16. Tel: 01635 42884. RG14 2BP

NEWBURY MARINA - Newbury, Kennet & Avon Canal, Map 16. Tel: 0758 456 6197. RG14 5SG

PENTON HOOK MARINA (MDL) - Penton Hook, River Thames, Map 39. Tel: 01932 568681. KT16 8PY

PORTAVON MARINA - Keynsham, River Avon, Map 2. Tel: 01225 424301. BS31 2DD

RACECOURSE MARINA (TINGDENE) - Windsor, River Thames, Map 37. 01753 910750. SL4 5HT

SALTFORD MARINA - Saltford, River Avon, Map 3. Tel: 01225 872226. BS31 3EZ

SEMINGTON DOCK - Semington, Kennet & Avon, Map 6. Tel: 01380 870654. BA14 6JT

SHEPPERTON MARINA - Shepperton, River Thames, Map 40. Tel: 01932 243722. TW17 8NS

SHERIDAN MARINE - Moulsford, River Thames, Map 27. Tel: 01491 652085. OX10 9HU

THAMES DITTON MARINA - Thames Ditton, River Thames, Map 41. Tel: 0208 398 6159. KT6 5QD

THAMES & KENNET MARINA (TINGDENE) - Caversham, River Thames, Maps 21 & 30. Tel: 0118 948 2911. RG4 6LQ

WALTON MARINA (TINGDENE) - Walton, River Thames, Map 40. Tel: 01932 226305. KT12 1QW

WINDSOR MARINA (MDL) - Windsor, River Thames, Map 36. Tel: 01753 853911. SL4 5TZ

VAL WYATT MARINE - Wargrave, River Thames, Map 32. Tel: 0118 940 3211. RG10 8LH

Day Boat Hire

ABINGDON BRIDGE MARINE - Abingdon, River Thames, Map 24. Tel: 01235 521125. OX14 3HX

BATH NARROWBOATS - Bath, Kennet & Avon Canal, Map 4. Tel: 01225 447276. BA2 4EL

CAVERSHAM BOAT SERVICES - Reading, R. Thames, Maps 21 & 30. Tel: 0118 957 4323. RG1 8DG

CHERTSEY MEADS MARINE - Chertsey, River Thames, Map 40. Tel: 01932 564699. KT16 8LN

DBH MARINE - Walton, River Thames, Map 40. Tel: 01483 224229. KT12 2PF

DEVIZES MARINA - Devizes, Kennet & Avon Canal, Map 8. Tel: 01380 725300. SN10 2RH

DITTON CRUISERS - Thames Ditton, River Thames, Map 41. Tel: 0208 398 2119. KT7 0QQ

HAMPTON FERRY - Hampton, River Thames, Map 41. Tel: 0208 979 7471. TW12 2EW

HARTS CRUISERS - Surbiton, River Thames, Map 42. Tel: 0208 398 2119. KT6 4HJ

HILPERTON MARINA - Hilperton, Trowbridge, Kennet & Avon Canal, Map 6. Tel: 01225 765243. BA14 8RS

HOBBS - Henley, River Thames, Map 32. Tel: 01491 572035. RG9 1AZ

KRIS CRUISERS - Datchet, River Thames, Map 37. Tel: 01753 543930. SL3 9BU

KENNET HORSE BOAT - Kintbury, Kennet & Avon, Map 15. Tel: 01488 658866. RG17 9UY

WILTSHIRE NARROWBOATS - Bradford-on-Avon, Kennet & Avon Canal, Map 5. Tel: 01869 340348. BA15 1LE

Skiff Hire

RICHMOND BRIDGE BOAT HIRE - Richmond, River Thames, Map 43. Tel: 0208 948 8270. TW9 1TH

THAMES SKIFF HIRE - Walton, River Thames, Map 40. Tel: 01932 232433. KT12 2DG

Punt Hire

BATH BOATING STATION - Bathwick, River Avon, Map 4. Tel: 01225 312900. BA2 6QE

CHERWELL BOAT HOUSE - Magdalen Bridge, Oxford, River Cherwell, Map 22. Tel: 01865 515978. OX2 6ST

SALTERS - Folly Bridge, Oxford, River Thames, Map 22. Tel: 01865 243421. OX1 4LA

THE TEN CANAL COMPANIONS

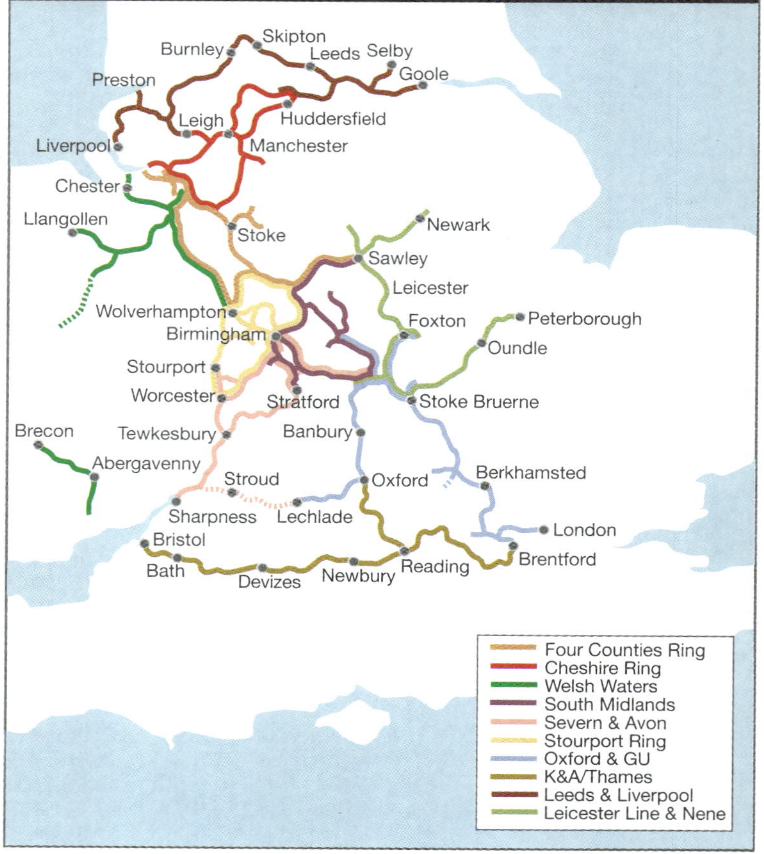